C000196235

MICHAEL BLANN

MOUNTAINS
EPIC CYCLING CLIMBS

173 ILLUSTRATIONS

Thames & Hudson

Contents

Monte Zoncolan: the start of the climb, and of gradients that reach 22 per cent.

Preface.
Michael Blann

The idea of photographing Europe's greatest climbs for a book arose from my love of cycling and my passion for photography. I grew up on the south coast of England and started racing in the 1980s during my teenage years, wowed by the first television coverage of the Tour de France. Like many youngsters, I had aspirations to be a professional cyclist, following in the footsteps of the riders I watched on television and read about in magazines. But after a year spent racing in Australia I realized it was not to be.

However, cycling has a habit of getting under one's skin, and it has remained a constant in my life. It's no surprise, then, that eventually it should have become the focus of my photography. Like all projects, it started as an inkling of an idea, followed by a short trip away to produce some 'personal work'. Little did I know at the time that it would evolve into a three-year project and a book from which I would learn so much.

For the last thirty years I had absorbed the history of the sport: I knew the names of the riders, the races and even all the famous climbs, but I had no connection with the physical landscape in which they raced. I didn't know the location of, say, the Col d'Izoard in relation to the Col du Galibier, nor the characteristics and terrain of each climb, so I set out to fill this void in my cycling knowledge.

Through this process of discovery I began creating a definitive record of these mountains within the context of cycling. Most of the cycling photography I had seen tended to focus on the action: it was shot from a motorbike, close-up or at the roadside. As a photographer, I have always preferred to shoot from afar. I naturally take the viewpoint of the passive observer looking over the wider scene as it unfolds before him. This detachment encourages a sense of quietness and deep introspection, which in turn is reflected in the final image. This may seem unfamiliar when we think of the melee of the Grand Tours, but even during race days the cacophony of the crowd lining the route can be muffled and swallowed up by the vastness of the mountain landscape, allowing natural sounds – meltwater, wind or rock falls – to emerge.

With this idea in mind, I set about photographing the races in their wider context. I wanted to document the permanence of these landforms, their relative scale and their sheer presence. I wanted to capture the unique character of every mountain – the roads and man-made structures that punctuated the landscape, its vegetation and the impact of the seasons.

While at first the book may appear to be a record of Alpine landscapes, underpinning this body of work is a study of how cyclists and the sport of cycling feel about mountains. Professional cycle racing is laced with drama and intrigue – an atmosphere that only intensifies during the mountain stages. Take, for example, the rivalry between the two great Italian riders Fausto Coppi and Gino Bartali in the Giro d'Italia, or the fierce duel on the Alpe d'Huez between teammates Bernard Hinault and Greg LeMond in the 1986 Tour de France.

This is the history of our sport, which leaves an indelible mark on our minds and, in turn, on our perception of the physical landscape where it was played out. As fans of cycling, we may view this theatre close-up at the roadside and feel part of the race, but in reality we are always at a distance. We are bystanders, present for only a short time; memories are fleeting, and details are forgotten soon after the event like a blip on the geological timescale, the cycle race is a travelling circus that visits for the day and then is gone, leaving the mountain, the constant, behind.

Over the course of this project I discovered that cycling has a symbiotic relationship with the mountains. These jagged peaks and cols provide a playground, a stage, for the drama that is professional cycling, and in return the race connects us back to the mountain landscape. There are many mountains, equally beautiful, that neighbour the great cycling climbs but, lacking in history or provenance, they have no purpose or meaning for cyclists. In short, they might as well not exist.

This work brings together my thoughts and visions, in what I hope is a comprehensive photographic record of cycling's greatest European climbs. It aims to explore the unique relationship between the physical landscape and cycling, paying homage to the sheer scale, physicality and changing moods of the mountains, and recognizing their importance in the history of the sport.

Introduction.
Susannah Osborne

It is impossible to talk about cycling without talking about mountains. For cyclists and fans of cycling, mountains are fundamental to understanding the nuances of the sport. Mont Ventoux, the Stelvio Pass, the Alpe d'Huez – these famous peaks have become temples where riders go to create a sense of self, where men and women validate their worth, and where the sport's heroes are born, and crushed.

There's something very primeval about making a passage over a mountain. From Hannibal to Napoleon, history tells us that these cols, peaks and summits present an immortal challenge to human physicality; their demanding gradients make us raw and challenge our self-belief. To conquer them demands a slice of your soul. As a cyclist, you leave a little bit of yourself on every mountain you ride.

For cyclists and spectators of cycling alike, our experiences of a landscape are intrinsic to a sense of place. The characteristics that make somewhere special help us to develop an affinity with, attach a story to, the physical environment. It follows that, for every cyclist – professional or amateur – each journey into and out of an Alpine landscape is distinct.

From the solitude imposed on the last man on the road, to the resolute descent of a rider dropped by the group and the deep suffering of a glycogen-depleted athlete, every ride is a deeply personal journey defined ultimately by the mountain.

There is a hierarchy of mountains, defined by the stories they have helped create and the punishments they have meted out. Gradients and lengths of climb lend them notoriety. And for every climber there is a tipping point. One mountain too far, one acceleration too hard, one bad day on the bike, and dreams and aspirations can melt away.

What the images included in this book show is that each mountain is unique, and that nothing stays the same: wind, rain, sunshine and snow can change and determine the experience and the climb.

What is also apparent is that cycling's imprint on the mountains is merely temporary. The Grand Tours bring a frenzy of fans, a cacophony of sound and a caravan of vehicles that fade when the race is over. As the last team cars descend off the mountain at breakneck speed, the crowds start to dissolve. As the sound of cheering stops and the energy and excitement generated by the race dissipate, a stillness returns; the pros were here and then, in an instant, they were gone. Even the memories, though still fresh in cycling's history, are gently erased by the evolution of this physical landscape. Save for the names imprinted in white paint on the road, it is as if they were never there.

Nature is indifferent to our obsession, and cycling is but one visitor to the mountains. We are allowed to stay only briefly, and on nature's terms: our ascents are limited by where the road goes, what the seasons will allow, and what the weather delivers at that specific moment. Yet the moment that the snows abate, the summits emerge, and the landscape allows cyclists increasingly to claim ownership of the space.

This sense of belonging has grown with the popularity of cycling and will no doubt continue to grow. The mountains call riders from all corners of the globe – cyclists desperate to identify with the struggle of riding against a gradient, riders who want to know what it's like to suffer.

Our experience of this physical realm would not have developed if it were not for technology. Television brought the mountain show to the masses, and now the digital sphere brings us even closer. In flat places far removed from any kind of Alpine landscape, riders rely on the virtual world to transport them to the mountains, where they can belong, despite their exile.

Technology brings us closer to the way professionals view the mountain landscape. We know the cyclists' speeds, their power; we see how they attack and how they descend. We gain real insights into the very personal experiences of some of the best and (by their own admission) most challenged climbers in the sport of cycling. What these stories show is that we all look differently at the same peak. With each and every summit we may develop a more complete understanding of ourselves, but our experiences are always unique. Ultimately, we can never predict how the story will end.

Col d'Allos: the Tour de France, 2015.

Col de l'Iseran: the route south towards Italy.

Northern French Alps

Col d'Izoard	*2,360 m*
Col de la Croix de Fer	*2,067 m*
Col du Galibier	**2,646 m**
Col du Lautaret	*2,057 m*
Lacets de Montvernier	*781 m*
Alpe d'Huez	**1,860 m**
Col de la Madeleine	*1,993 m*
Col de l'Iseran	**2,770 m**
Col du Mont Cenis	*2,081 m*

featuring contributions by
Michael Blann, Stephen Roche, Andy Hampsten, Paul Sherwen

Col d'Izoard: the road breaks out of the tree line at 2,000 m.

Col d'Izoard: the summit and the descent south towards Guillestre.

Col d'Izoard: the barren slopes of the Casse Déserte.

Stagiaire.
Michael Barry

They chatted as they smoked, in a language that was undecipherable. The air in the car was thick with diesel fuel and strong cigarettes. It was a Lada, or Skoda, or something from the East; I didn't pay attention, or I can't remember. My memories are spotty, as if the cold had frozen my thoughts. We drove down the final metres of the pass, into the wooded valley, towards the feed zone where, if I were still on my bike, I could have warmed up, pulled on a jacket and ploughed on towards the finish line in Le Grand Bornand.

The wipers tried to keep up with the snow that was accumulating on the windscreen. I was curled in the corner, against the passenger door, snuggled – no, jammed – between the mechanic, the spare wheels, his toolbox, a dozen water bottles and a team's worth of musettes. On the mountain road thin lines left by bicycle tyres were etched into the snow, like threads in a fairy tale for the driver to follow. I gazed out the window, frozen in defeat.

At the top, before I quit, I was already cold, and a blanket of snow covered the road. I'd asked a TV motorcyclist whether I could borrow his gloves, just for a minute, as I prepared myself for the 20 km descent. Without pity, he said, 'No.'

Bicycles, with their frame numbers and shimmering paintwork, were piled outside the summit café, their colours contrasting with the stone building, the snow-piled roof and the greyness that had closed in. I wasn't going to join them, my rivals, in the warm café; I wasn't going to quit. In front of me on the snow-covered road was my opportunity to fulfil a goal, a dream: I was in the top ten in the Tour de l'Avenir, and the professional *directeurs* were taking note. This was the penultimate stage. A contract would come, I was sure. The mountains make champions. And they crush cyclists…

On the start line, I had mapped out the day in my head. Ominous clouds loomed overhead, a shroud moving in to squelch the joy of the crowd. Being Canadian, I would overcome the cold rain, I thought. But I was unprepared on every level: I wore only Lycra shorts, a thin jersey and arm warmers. I didn't even have a waterproof jacket. The loudspeakers boomed Gloria Gaynor's 'I Will Survive', which would haunt me long after I had climbed off my bike.

It was the longest climb I had ever raced: 20.3 km and 1,227 m of ascent. The peloton shattered early on, and a break had gone up the road. This meant that the team at the front of the chasing group, ONCE, was setting a tempo that had us digging in. A sign said '20 km au sommet'. I tried to ignore it. At the pace we were riding, few riders would hold onto the leaders for even 2 km. Then we would be alone or in small groups until the summit, which was hours away.

The road narrowed as we climbed into the trees. The tarmac was rough, a chip seal that dug into the tyres, slowing us, making the fight even tougher. Rain was now turning to snow. Between breaths, pants, riders shook their heads: 'What are we doing?' There was no talk of calling the race off. We were too young and naive to protest at racing in such conditions.

It had collapsed into a race of survival. A peloton of young boys, all under 25, who would otherwise be at university, working in a factory or ploughing a field, were pushing up a mountainside with four passes to climb before the finish. We were together as a group but alone in our effort, all because we wanted something greater: to be professional racing cyclists tearing over mountains in the Tour de France. We were on our way to achieving the dream, and now was not the time to give in.

I had moved to the French Alps to race as an amateur when I was 20, but despite my youth I was already starting to ride and feel the way my heroes did, or so I thought. I had that sensation of flight – when the bike moves fluidly beneath the rider for an hour, swaying as he rides out of the saddle, ticking like a metronome as he sits firmly back down, his breath in time with his legs and the potency of the pedal stroke, increasing only as he snakes through the switchbacks.

In cycling nothing is comparable to climbing. And that may be true for life in general. Many of my finest days have been on a bicycle in the mountains. As a child, small hills were my Alpine passes; the feeling of arriving at the top, having pedalled to get there, was unparalleled.

The mechanic butted his cigarette out in the ashtray and held me tight, shaking me to get the blood flowing. On his breath I could smell booze laced with cigarettes. I felt the grease on his hands but I didn't push him off; I was too tired, too dismayed, and the human touch was comforting and consoling. I closed my eyes, delirious from the cold, not wanting to admit that my race was over.

He had stopped with his *directeur sportif* after passing me on the descent. Like most pro cyclists desperate to make it to the line, I said, 'No, I'm going to keep going.' They pulled me off my bike, insisting that I stop, for fear I would lose more than just a bike race. Hours later I woke in another car, the Canadian team van, parked outside the team hotel. Over one hundred riders had started the race but fewer than forty had finished.

Three-and-a-half months before, I'd been watching the Tour de France on television in a German hotel room, with my Canadian teammate Steve Bauer. We were preparing for the Atlanta Olympics. I was a young amateur; Bauer was an old pro. As the race went up and over the summit of the Cormet de Roselend, the commentators listed the riders and their time gaps. Ullrich, Riis, Virenque, Escartin, Leblanc…It was 1996. They were flying.

On television it looked easy. I could be there with them, I thought. Bauer had ridden fourteen Tours, had been placed fourth once, and had worn the yellow jersey several times. His commentary was unlike any other: he knew the riders personally and seemed to recognize every kilometre of tarmac. As the group – a few dozen riders – threaded their way down the sinuous wet mountainside, he told me that there was a dangerous corner coming up and that crashes happened at that spot.

Moments later, a rider missed the corner and shot off the road, sailing and then disappearing into the dense trees. The commentators were in shock. Steve said nothing, his eyes wide with fear for a compatriot. Within seconds, motorcyclists and team cars had stopped. They were pulling a rider out of the bushes ten metres or more down the embankment: #81, Johan Bruyneel. Having dodged death and with barely a scratch, he climbed on a spare bike and sped off in pursuit of the group.

Months later, I saw the same corner as I raced up and over the mountain in the Tour de l'Avenir. Under the falling snow I thought, 'We are always at the mercy of the mountains, no matter how good or fit we are.' Cyclists learn, with experience, to respect the mountains. There are few passes that haven't marked me in body and in spirit. The good and bad memories stay, as do the scars I bear from the crashes that occurred as I hurtled down the descents. The trophies are now in cabinets, and boxes of memories mark the mountains I triumphed on. I remember the gear ratios I rode, the riders I was with, the weather that seared our skin or froze our bones, and the times I bonked and buckled under the efforts. And I remember when I flew, amazing myself that I could travel so fast.

Those contrasts are what build the adventure. On a mountainside, a cyclist can pedal a rhythm that focuses his thoughts. He can let his breath set his pace with a smooth intensity and find serenity in the effort. For that, I will pedal up mountains until I am too old or broken to climb on a bicycle.

Col de la Croix de Fer: the 'Pass of the Iron Cross'.

Col de la Croix de Fer: looking back towards the Col du Glandon.

Col de la Croix de Fer: some of the 250 vehicles that make up the publicity caravan on the Tour de France.

Northern French Alps.

Col du Galibier.

2,646 m

Stephen Roche

It was Stage 21 of the 1987 Tour, from Bourg-d'Oisans to La Plagne. There were three climbs that day, and the Colombians attacked as soon as we hit the first one, the Galibier: [Luis] Herrera, [Fabio] Parra and the Café de Colombia team, they just took off.

There were crashes, guys went down, but they didn't let up. They didn't do the sporting thing and wait, they just pushed on, riding tempo. Because it was early on in the stage, we tried to get them to back off – 'Piano, piano' – telling them to slow; we knew riders would be eliminated if they carried on pushing hard and that wasn't a fair way to ride. But they didn't stop.

Towards the top of the Galibier, the contenders for the general classification– Jean-François Bernard, Charly Mottet, Pedro Delgado and I – were all there, and we began to talk. If we waited until the next climb, the Madeleine, and the Colombians did the same again, we'd run the risk of getting dropped, so we made a pact: 'Let's make them ride downhill.'

Descending is an art. To take a descent fast, you have to know where to break and which line to take. You need to understand about weight transfer and how your body moves on the bike.

The descent off the Galibier was crazy. It was so, so fast. We rode together as a pack, took huge risks, took the corners like madmen, but we were mostly in control. The road is narrow in places, there are long stretches without barriers, so one mistake and that would have been it. But it worked; that descent blew them out, and they never came back.

My memories from that stage are so vivid. I drove the Galibier in a rally car not long after I retired, and I remembered the corners, their gradients and the road furniture just as they were. There's a sharp left-hand bend with a high wall running around it about 3 km from the summit. I remembered that this was the start of the final effort to reach the top. I'd kept a picture of it in my mind for all those years, and I'll never forget that corner. It's where we came up with our plan.

Col du Galibier: snow clings to the northern slopes in summer.

Col du Galibier: the jagged peaks of the Dauphiné Alps.

Col du Galibier: according to Henri Desgrange, compared to the Galibier all other climbs were 'gnat's piss'.

Col du Galibier: the bridge and hairpin bend mark the steepest sections of the ascent.

Col du Galibier: the long grind to Plan Lachat from Valloire.

Col du Galibier: the last rider in the general classification of the Tour de France is called the 'lanterne rouge',
a reference to the red lantern that was used to guide riders at night during the first few editions of the race.

Col du Galibier: the 'Souvenir Henri Desgrange' is awarded to the first rider over the summit, in memory of the founder of the Tour de France.

Dark Days.
Stephen Roche

There's a saying that the Tour leaves you, but you never leave the Tour.

It happened at the base of the Hautacam, in the 1986 Tour. I'd just come back from a knee injury and was well down on both the stage and the GC [general classification]. The pain in my knee was excruciating, and as I approached the climb it became too much to bear. I rode over an old stone bridge, slowed down and climbed off my bike. Sitting there at the side of the road I'd given up; in my mind the stage and my Tour were over.

I'd been there for a few minutes when an old man came over to me. 'Roche, what are you doing?' he said. I replied, in French, 'I can't do it, I'm just so tired, I'll never get to the top of Hautacam.'

'A rider like you, you have to go on. Have some water and get back on your bike.'

I told him I was injured and that I was in pain, but all he said was, 'You have to go on.' So I gave him my Carrera cap, swung my leg over the bike and rode on. By the end I was in a terrible state but I'd finished.

The following year I won the Tour de France. The penultimate stage was a time trial in Dijon, won by Jean-François Bernard. As I went over the line I caught a glimpse of a man wearing a white Carrera cap: it was the man from the bridge. We spoke, and I thanked him for his support on that day. In a quiet voice and with complete certainty, he simply said, 'You were right to go on.'

I wasn't a natural climber; I became a climber by learning to climb, for that I've got Robert Millar to thank. Stage 18 of the 1983 Tour finished on the Joux Plane, just outside Morzine. It was my first Tour, so every day was a big deal for me. I'd made it into a chasing group with Millar and, when he attacked from the group, I managed to get across. I sat on his wheel all the way to the finish.

I watched everything that Millar did: how his body moved, the way he pedalled. His cadence hardly changed all the way up; he established his rhythm and rode to it, tapping out the pedal strokes one by one. Robert stayed in the saddle and rarely stood up, backed off going into the corners so that he could ride hard out of them, and made it look effortless. Easy.

My gaze was fixed on his wheel for the whole of that 11 km climb – I knew I couldn't lose it. We came in at exactly the same time, but the difference between us was that where I'd been simply hanging on, he'd been climbing. But by hanging on I was forced to watch and observe, and I learnt so much. Until then I had just ridden up the climbs, but on that day I became a climber, which meant that I could be a true contender in the Grand Tours.

Every climber has his weak points. I knew that if I rode an erratic ride I wouldn't get to the top, so for me it was about being calm and consistent. My 1987 ride up to La Plagne was a game of cat and mouse. Pedro Delgado knew how I rode. He knew that, if he attacked a couple of times and I went with him, it would finish me off, so that's exactly what he tried to do. He attacked immediately, and I had to let him go because if I went with him I wouldn't see the top. I had to keep my cool, but in my head I was constantly thinking, 'How far can I let him go? How many times will I let him attack?'

On climbs like the Alpe d'Huez, with its steep corners, Delgado would kill me; even with the yellow jersey on my back I lost 2 minutes to Delgado on that climb. But on a consistent climb I could be myself, ride in my style, and that's what I did on La Plagne. I let him get a minute, then 1 minute and 10 seconds, 1 minute and 20, but at some point I had to stop the gap getting any bigger. It was a guessing game: had he blown up or bottomed out, or did he have more to give? To win the Tour I needed to get within 30 seconds of him, but there were no reliable time checks and the team car was behind. What's more, with the crowds surrounding you it was impossible to hear anything. I waited until there was 4 km to go and buried myself from there to the finish. It was only when I came around the final corner with 200 m to go that I saw Delgado. Then I knew I'd done it, I played the right game.

Col du Lautaret: overshadowed by the early slopes of the Col du Galibier.

Lacets de Montvernier: sometimes described as an Alpine Scalextric, the climb has eighteen hairpins that switch back every 150 m.

Lacets de Montvernier: the slope was closed to spectators, team cars and the publicity caravan during its inaugural appearance in the 2015 Tour de France.

Northern French Alps.

Alpe d'Huez.

1,860 m

Andy Hampsten

The road to the Alpe d'Huez is so unspectacular, it's one of my least favourite climbs, but it's a real theatre for cycling. It's wide, made so that tourists can drive on snowy roads to go skiing, but fill it with people and cyclists and it becomes a party.

Racing up d'Huez is fantastic. There's an insane amount of energy that comes from the crowd. It's overhyped, which makes it way more stressful than it needs to be, but overall it's the best stage of the Tour de France, which is already an overhyped, full-on bike race.

As a climb it might not be the toughest, and it's probably rated 'hors catégorie' only because the race finishes there, but during the Tour it becomes like the World Championships for climbers. That day in 1992 when I won on the Alpe, I wanted to protect my place in the general classification, but overall the stage win was more important.

I don't like the climb's first kilometres so I'd planned to make my move in the last third. Two of the guys in the group, Jan Evans and Jesús Montoya, dropped off early on. As we approached the steeper hairpins I accelerated

hard, seated in the saddle and spinning to make it look like I was just feeling good.

At this point Éric Boyer dropped away and Franco Vona lost two or three bike lengths. I kept the pressure on so that Vona had to claw back each metre to reach me, but he couldn't. It had worked.

It's easy to get carried away on the Alpe d'Huez – the crowds, the win, it means so much – but I saved a little bit for the final 3 km. This last kick is hard: the road undulates and the crowd gets thicker and thicker.

In 1989 my entire team had food poisoning on the stage to the Alpe d'Huez. It was on this day that Eddy Merckx, our new sponsor, chose to go in the team car. He said to me, 'Andy, I'm going to follow you and watch you win on the Alpe d'Huez.' I finished 84th on that stage; I started in the front group and finished at the back, but I gave 100 per cent knowing that Merckx was in the car behind me. After the stage he got out and said, 'Tomorrow's a new day. Don't you say a word, I understand perfectly.' In 1992 I drew on that day and imagined Merckx in the car behind me. I won.

Alpe d'Huez: there are twenty-one hairpins to negotiate before cyclists reach the ski station.

Alpe d'Huez: with the party over, the crowds begin to disperse.

Alpe d'Huez: arguably the most iconic climb in the Tour de France.

Above: Alpe d'Huez, 'Dutch Corner': Joop Zoetemelk inspired the Dutch love affair with the Alpe.
Right: Alpe d'Huez: the valley road from Grenoble to Bourg-d'Oisans.

The Climber.
Paul Sherwen

I saw my first mountain range when I rode my first Tour de France. I grew up in East Africa; we had mountains, but they seemed far, far away, in a distant place at the end of the plains. Seeing these mountains for the first time was a shock.

I got an inkling pretty early on in my career that the mountains weren't for me. Those first experiences in the Alps and Pyrenees were terrible, soul-destroying; I couldn't stay in the pack or even stay in touch. I was on my own. But I realized that I needed to find a way of coping. I still had to make it to the line.

I'd been to university and I was good at maths, which meant that I could calculate the elimination times down to the second. The night before a mountain stage, I'd work out how fast I had to ride and for how long. I'd write it down on a piece of card and then lodge the numbers in my head. It was critical for me to know exactly how hard I had to ride and how far I had to climb, and it's still that critical for many in the Tour de France now.

There were days when there were twenty or thirty riders in the autobus at the back of the race, but the stages that stand out – the ones that I'll never forget – are when I was alone, off the back, struggling to breathe, struggling to turn the pedals, struggling to stay in the race. On days like those I had an image in my mind: I'd see a railway barrier slowly coming down on the finish line. I had to make it to the line and duck my head under the barrier to be safe, and I usually did.

Despite the struggle I knew that the mountains were part of the job. You have to ride them even if you loathe them, because they are such an important part of the Grand Tours. There were times when the mountains broke me. During the 1983 Tour de France I was climbing the Col de la Madeleine. I had bronchitis and was sick. I remember looking up at this mountain 2,000 m high and feeling crushed, so I climbed off. I was beaten.

My nickname was 'The Climber'. It was a joke because I was always the first one to get dropped, but I was a good guy to be with because the other riders knew that it was pretty certain I'd make it inside the time limit. If we were off the back, the team car would come past us and hand us a pump and a spare tyre, and it was 'Good luck, mate.'

The memories of some of those stages are hazy, but others are still fresh in my mind. In the 1980 Tour we were climbing the Alpe d'Huez. I was alongside Allan Peiper. We were both at the limit of our physical capabilities. When you're in that state you can be irrational, do stupid stuff; it encourages you. In the 1980s there were Dutch supporters all the way up the climb, not just at Dutch Corner – they took the place over, they owned it, and they would push the Dutch riders. One guy pushed a rider and then stopped in the road. Allan couldn't go anywhere and rode into him, and then he just lost it.

There's a brick wall on the right-hand side of the climb. I looked over and saw Allan with this guy pinned up against the wall. He was beating the shit out of him. I dragged him off and urged him to get back on the bike, so we could make the cut. At that point he just snapped, he was crying and sobbing, so I had to talk him all the way up the climb to avoid elimination. We weren't even on the same team: he was riding for Peugeot and I was riding for La Redoute. [Luis] Herrera the Colombian won that day, but I doubt he experienced the Alpe like we did. We were just inside the time limit.

The next day we started at the bottom of the Alpe d'Huez in Bourg-d'Oisans and went straight over the Galibier. It's a horrible, long, brutal climb of nearly 20 km. The Colombians – Delgado, Herrera – came out of the starting blocks and went ballistic from the gun. The group was lined out and going crazy. At one point Sean Yates sat up and shouted, 'You're all bleedin' idiots!' The men at the front couldn't hear that, but at least he got it off his chest. Then Yates, who was riding next to Peiper, looked across at him and said, 'Don't worry. The Climber's behind you.' And I was.

It was one of those days when I had real doubts about whether we were going to make it. The stage finished at the top of La Plagne, another long climb. To get to the line on days like that you have to take risks; there were six of us at the back taking turns on the flat and running serious risks on the descent; we took the corners tight, rode too fast. In those days the spectators listened to the race on radios at the side of the road. We could hear who had won the stage – it was Laurent Fignon – but it was still 17 km to the end, and I knew we had 27 minutes in which to get there. Peiper and I were together – the d'Huez stage had bonded us – but it was one of those days when I could see the barrier coming down. We rode harder and harder and just ducked our heads under.

Col de la Madeleine: at over 24 km, this is one of the longest Alpine climbs.

Col de l'Iseran.

2,770 m

Michael Blann

It was a sweltering hot day during the 1992 Tour as I waited with thousands of fans on the final climb to Sestriere for the race to arrive. Groups of men were huddled around portable radios listening to the stage unfold. Snippets of information crackled over the airwaves: a breakaway had gone clear near the very start of the stage, a mammoth 250 km away. On paper it was suicidal, but the group was made up of some notable names: Sean Kelly, Raúl Alcalá, Richard Virenque, Thierry Claveyrolat and, most importantly, Claudio Chiappucci, who was the biggest threat to the general classification.

This was only my second time watching the Tour on the roadside, and I was a novice compared with the veteran tour fans who followed the race every year. As the temperature soared, I sought out the shade of a tree and rationed the water in my bidon with one, slow sip at a time (it was going to be a long day). Back on the course Chiappucci was slowly turning the screws, shelling riders out the back on each of the climbs. By the time he hit the Col de l'Iseran, only Virenque was left, and halfway up the 37 km climb he was gone too.

Chiappucci was strong, relying on his muscular physique to keep the gears ticking over; he didn't have the grace or finesse of a pure climber, yet he ticked off the climbs one by one. From the top of the Col de l'Iseran, Europe's highest pass, Chiappucci would be able to see Italy on the horizon. A home win was on the cards, and Italian fans were already in a celebratory mood.

For a long time no information came through, and the anticipation was palpable. Then, finally, the drone of the Tour helicopters coming over the mountain caught my attention: the wait was over.

The crowd swarmed into the road to catch the first glimpse of the race. As the first rider came into view, we tracked his progress up the climb. The crowd, four people deep, separated, and through the cacophony Chiappucci emerged, his eyes sunken, his face drawn, his polka-dot jersey and shorts stained by salt tides. And then, in a moment, he was gone.

One by one, riders ground their way up the climb. Miguel Indurain, Franco Vona, Gianni Bugno and Andy Hampsten fared the best, but most had succumbed to the heat and were on a death march towards the finish line. A group containing the three-times Tour winner Greg LeMond eventually rolled past some fifty minutes later, outside the time limit and out of the Tour.

At the time I felt cheated – the wait seemed disproportionate compared to the few glimpses I'd had of the riders – but, looking back, I've come to appreciate that I was part of something historic. That day's events have been etched on my brain: the crowds, the wait, the sunburn, the physical distress of the riders. It was brutal. Stephen Roche once confessed, 'It was the hardest day I spent on a bike.'

When I visited the Col de l'Iseran to photograph it for this book, I imagined Chiappucci and all the other riders coming over the crest and looking at the view towards Italy. It became apparent that there is a symbiotic relationship between the mountains and the races. The mountains provide a platform on which to create history, and in return the racing and Grand Tours give significance back to the mountains. It's what draws us to the mountains to follow in the footsteps of our heroes.

Col de l'Iseran: Europe's highest paved pass.

Col de l'Iseran: the first mountain time trial took place on the Col de l'Iseran in 1939.

Col de l'Iseran: this climb provided the springboard for Claudio Chiappucci's daring 125 km escape and stage win in the 1992 Tour de France.

Col de l'Iseran: originally a mule pass, the road was officially opened in 1937.

Col de l'Iseran: the road took thirty-four years to complete.

Col de l'Iseran: the summit, looking north to Val d'Isère and south towards Italy.

Col de l'Iseran: the chapel of Notre-Dame de Toute-Prudence.

Col du Mont Cenis: the Musée de la Pyramide overlooks the dam.

Col du Mont Cenis: the road over the pass was built by Napoleon in 1803–10.

Col du Mont Cenis: the large reservoir dominates the plateau at the summit.

Col du Mont Cenis: three riders tackle the last few ramps on the Italian side.

Col de la Cayolle: early morning on the lower slopes.

Southern French Alps

Col d'Allos	2,250 m
Col de la Bonette	**2,715 m**
Col de la Cayolle	2,326 m
Col des Champs	2,087 m
Mont Ventoux	**1,912 m**

featuring contributions by Romain Bardet, Robert Millar, Greg LeMond

Col d'Allos: a helicopter tracks the Tour de France's progress for television.

Col d'Allos: the Mavic neutral support car follows the breakaway.

Liberty.
Romain Bardet

Each year, after the chaos of racing in the mountain stages, I feel the need to go back to the Alps to ride, just me against the mountain in all its beautiful summer glory.

It's impossible to appreciate the true value of the mountains when you're riding the Tour. Their breadth, the harmony and tranquillity of the place, panoramas so full of riches that don't register when the stakes are high. In a race, the supreme happiness that comes from climbing is always trumped by the need to win.

These rides, after the season has ended, are my favourite outings. Being alone with my bike at dawn, when the air is cool and crisp, is a reminder that I'm high up, at altitude. You carry the bare minimum: a windcheater on your back, a bidon of water, and 20 Euros in your back pocket. This kind of riding is raw.

This is the time when you can make your bike dance to the rhythm of the road. There's a joy that comes from negotiating the twists and turns of a mountain pass, but that feeling of jubilation doesn't come free: it's payback for those gruelling weeks of altitude training in the spring.

This thirst for the summits and these moments of two-wheeled freedom are priceless, synonymous with the joy of summertime, of 'letting go' after the endurance and discipline demanded by months of racing.

The first time I rode like this was unforgettable. Emerging from the Tour de France, worn out by the media madness of those three weeks, we decided to go out as a group of friends to ride the mountains around Val d'Isère. Free from the constraints of a successful season, my health was sparkling. Finally, after weeks of holding back, I could make the most of my legs and ride as I wanted, for me.

As we approached each climb, it was as if the mountain were pulling me up. I couldn't stop myself surging forward, embracing each metre of altitude that lay before me on the tarmac. The endorphins swirling round my body seemed to multiply with each metre we climbed. At the summit we stopped, relaxed, drank coffee and ate freshly cooked crêpes in a moment of intense friendship.

During these 'holidays', my favourite climb was the Col de l'Iseran from the ski station at Val d'Isère; the Alpine countryside is distinctive, the tarmac perfect, and the changes in gradient incessant. It's a real treat for the purists.

Ahead of me was an uphill speed interval session; I needed to get my body used to the changes in pace that characterize the end-of-season races. My initial plan was for a 30-minute training session, but I couldn't resist: I kept the exercise going right to the summit at 2,700 m. I'd been intoxicated by the feeling of speed, lured by the rhythmic changes of the climb. Cycling is not all about calibrated training; this spontaneity is the true essence of our sport.

These rides shape me: they are part of a journey, a path, and at the end of that path is the rider that I hope to become. It's these rides and this feeling of liberty that sow the seed for those spontaneous breaks and lone attacks that occur during races.

The climb, and the descent, of the Col d'Allos in the 2015 Critérium du Dauphiné were the realization of these heady desires to open up the mountain road, the pack chasing behind. This beautiful mountain with a unique aura, little known before the race, gave me an opportunity.

At the foot of the hill I felt claustrophobic and oppressed by the group, so I devised a plan to escape. 'One attack, just one, to reach the summit alone in the lead': the words went round my head. 'Then throw yourself headlong into the descent,' I told myself. 'Take the risks, experience those unique sensations that come with riding fast and at the edge of control.'

The screeching of the lead car's tyres were a wake-up call and a reminder that I was flirting with the limits of reason; a mountain descent is a test where, perched on two wheels, we can keep up with cars that have ten times the power.

A straight route interrupted by a steep cliff and a parapet edge, protection from an abyss that is as deep as it is threatening: we have been warned to take care. Yet I know I can take advantage of this evil reputation, so I make a decision to approach this descent in the lead. I can exploit the fears of the group and use them to my advantage.

What came next was a solitary climb, a chase, a hunt by a ferocious yellow-jersey group so hungry that only a win would keep them happy. That's the price of victory in the mountains, but still I want more.

Col d'Allos: the hair-raising descent back towards Barcelonnette.

Southern French Alps.

Col de la Bonette.

2,715 m

Robert Millar.

I like climbing, but 24 km uphill and 2,860 m of altitude is daunting even when you are motivated and have a plan (first to the top).

It's rare to get the chance to challenge yourself with all that Col de la Bonette has to offer. The top is closed for most of the year, and it's not a regular occurrence in any race. The Tour de France has been up here just twice before, and, enticingly, on both occasions Federico Bahamontes was first to the summit. The rarity of the occasion appeals, as much as the honour of being added to a rather selective list.

As we come out of Jausiers and head towards the Bonette, the ride has vaguely followed the expected scenario – a mixture of hiding, waiting and suffering on the earlier climbs of Col d'Izoard and Col de Vars while enduring the dictated pace. So far I've been through the whole range of available emotions, from comfortable to worried. Confident was a fleeting companion somewhere in the middle.

The brief flat before the trouble really starts is dispatched at warp speed. The bigger guys in the group pull us along as if the finish were waiting round the corner. That all changes when we pass the board signalling the beginning of the climb, and as they come tumbling backwards it's time to go.

One minute later I have a 20-second lead, with only Pedro Delgado able to follow. The plan might just be on; I'll ride 10 km hard and see what happens. On a normal Col that would put me close to the top, but here it won't even be halfway. Strangely, it seems a reasonable thing to do.

Pedro is huffing and puffing to stay with me. I must be going fast if, despite the heat and almost two weeks of racing in my legs, he's hurting. Then suddenly he lets go and I'm on my own. Now what?

It's already high here, over 2,000 m, so anything down in the valley – such as team cars and riders – are just specks. Thankfully, now there are bends to break up the monotony and increase the sense of climbing. The gradient isn't as steady as it was before, but it's almost a relief to get out of the saddle, and I think I can see a summit. Probably not the actual summit, but it'll do as a focal point.

With 4 km remaining, the old Casernes de Restefond swings into view. I'm reassured that, barring a complete meltdown, I'm going to be summiting first. But I remember that the roadbook says the worst bit is waiting. I calm myself and change down a gear for the steepest bends. It's a wise tactic, for as I swing onto the final section, the Cime, the gradient, the altitude and the accumulated fatigue of the last 23 km all combine into a red-faced fight to the line. This hurts, but the plan has worked. Bahamontes and now me. Cool. I like the sound of that. The view's not bad either.

Col de la Bonette: the barren landscape looking back towards Jausiers

Col de la Bonette: a gateway to the south of France and the Côte d'Azur.

Col de la Bonette: the loop of the Cime de la Bonette.

Col de la Bonette: a favourite climb of Federico Bahamontes, first over the summit in both the 1962 and 1964 Tours.

Col de la Bonette: in 2008 John-Lee Augustyn crashed over the edge while leading the stage in the Tour de France.

Col de la Bonette: the road cuts through black shale rock.

Col de la Bonette: a lone rider tackles the 24 km ascent.

Above: Col de la Cayolle: two riders approach the summit.
Right: Col de la Cayolle: a bridge crosses the steep ravine and river below.

Col des Champs: the road meanders through Alpine forest for much of the ascent.

Col des Champs: the grey shale summit.

Mont Ventoux.

1,912 m

Greg LeMond

Ventoux is one of those climbs that left a lasting impression; for me, cycling on Mont Ventoux and the summer are what road cycling is about.

I was 19 years old and in my first year as a pro, riding the Dauphiné. The Ventoux was my first experience of a truly big 'hors catégorie' climb, and as we rode up from Malaucène I was finding it tough; I suffered from allergies during the summer months, so my eyes were swollen and I was finding it hard to breathe. I remember feeling a sense of panic as I gasped for breath.

Bernard Hinault had already won five stages of the race and I was third in the GC [general classification], but on that day he was a good teammate: he pushed me a couple of times when I was finding it really tough. Being able to stick with Hinault was confirmation that, despite not being on top form, I wasn't far off my best and could stay with the top riders.

Three years later I did the Dauphiné again. I was in the yellow jersey with Pascal Simon from Peugeot just behind me in the GC. It was dry and really hot, over 90°F [32°C], just like you imagine the Ventoux to be, with a heat haze coming off the white limestone and that fierce Mistral wind whipping up the dust. I loved the heat – that's what I thrived on, and it was just like California, where I grew up.

On that day I was feeling superb, and I attacked Pascal Simon right at the bottom, just outside Bédoin before you hit the forest. Simon came back to me, and so we rode together, swapping turns on the front.

But then, towards the mid-section, he kicked and performed a massive sprint. He was in his big chain ring, riding away from me up a steep climb. I tried to follow him but I just couldn't do it, and I blew up. It was the first time I've ever blown like that on a climb. I lost a minute and a half that day, and the yellow jersey. Maybe I was a little over-confident, but he was so incredibly strong.

I wish we could have raced Ventoux in the Tour de France but sadly I never did. I have the greatest respect for the climbs where I suffered the most, and on Ventoux I really did suffer.

Mont Ventoux: the Giant of Provence

Mont Ventoux: the most popular ascent, from Bédoin.

Mont Ventoux: the Paris–Nice, Critérium du Dauphiné and Tour de France races are all frequent visitors to the mountain.

Mont Ventoux: tree-felling by Toulon shipbuilders has left the upper slopes above Chalet Reynard bare.

Mont Ventoux: limestone scree offers little protection from the mistral and intense summer heat.

Mont Ventoux: the iconic telecommunications mast, built in the 1960s, marks the finish line.

Mont Ventoux the night before a Tour visit.

Col du Tourmalet: the ski station at La Mongie coming into view.

Pyrenees

featuring contributions by
Paul Sherwen, Sean Kelly, Bernie Eisel, Geraint Thomas, Robert Millar

Port de Balès: riders tackle the fast descent into Bagnères-de-Luchon.

Port de Balès: the scene of 'Chaingate', in which Andy Schleck dropped his chain in the 2010 Tour de France.

Port de la Bonaigua: poles to mark the depth of snow line the road.

Port de la Bonaigua: horses roam wild in the pastures surrounding the mountain.

Col de Peyresourde at first light.

Col de Peyresourde has made over fifty appearances in the Tour de France.

Pyrenees.
Col d'Aubisque.
1,709 m

Paul Sherwen

In the 1985 Tour de France we went over the Aubisque twice in one day. There was a short morning stage of 52.5 km and then an afternoon stage of 83.5 km, with lunch in between. They'd never do that now.

I'd already experienced the Aubisque; in a previous tour I was dropped going on the climb from Pau. On the long scar that runs from the summit towards the Col du Soulor I tried to make up time. It was foggy, raining, and the roads were damp. I was taking wild lines but there's no safety barrier.

You do crazy things on a bike sometimes, things there's no way you could have rehearsed. I went around a corner and I knew I wasn't going to make it, so I decked the bike, just dropped it on the tarmac. I was still in my toe clips, attached to the bike, sliding towards a cliff edge. I hit the concrete parapet, which was all that stopped me from falling 300 m down the mountain.

In 1985 we all knew that this day was all about Stephen Roche. Raphael Géminiani [team manager of La Redoute] had been talking him up all year to win that first stage, which finished at the top of the Aubisque. He'd told him to attack from the gun and treat it like a time trial. Stephen was even wearing a skin suit – something that had raised a few eyebrows.

Géminiani was old school – he'd been Jacques Anquetil's confidant and coach – and he'd play psychological games with Roche. He used to marinate fresh fish especially for him; Stephen would have a special plate of fish every day on that tour, while the team had beans and spaghetti.

Although we were teammates, my major concern wasn't helping Stephen. I was 8 or 9 minutes down on the winning time, and it wasn't far to go to Paris. I needed to get inside the time limit to survive, so, for me, riding the Aubisque was simply about making the cut. In this stage it was everyone for themselves, and he knew he wasn't going to get any help from me.

Col d'Aubisque: one of two tunnels through the Cirque du Litor.

Col d'Aubisque: night falls as low cloud envelopes the summit.

Col d'Aubisque: the café and souvenir shop mark the top.

Above: Col d'Aubisque: the section where the climb meets the Col du Soulor.
Right: Col d'Aubisque: Wim van Est was rescued with the help of forty tyres fastened together after he plunged over the side in the 1951 Tour while wearing the yellow jersey.

Col d'Aubisque: along with the Col du Tourmalet, the Col de Peyresourde and the Col d'Aspin,
this mountain forms the stage known as the 'Circle of Death'.

Col d'Aubisque: the Cirque du Litor.

Day in Yellow.
Sean Kelly

Your genes are what determine if you are a good climber, and that's something that you simply can't change; the natural climbers are lightweight little fellas, the ones who weigh less than 60 kg.

While it's true to say that everyone can improve their climbing ability through training, if you're not blessed with the natural physique, you'll never be great in the mountains. Robert Millar was the perfect example of a small guy who made climbing look easy. Roche had good climbing ability but he wasn't a natural climber; Stephen was there to get through the mountains. He had the grit and the determination to get to the top, but he'd often lose a bit in the final kilometres, and that's the difference.

When you do a lot of Grand Tours your memories of those mountain stages get muddled up. I climbed the Alpe d'Huez six times, but I can't remember the difference between those six stages. In fact there was no difference; it was always bloody torture. What's more, when you're climbing it on a normal day outside of the Tour it's not a spectacular climb, the views aren't impressive and there's no magnificent scenery. There's not a lot to mark it out.

Back in the 1980s the Alpe d'Huez always came at the end of a long stage. You could have ridden 200 km and still have to climb the Alpe. When you're 72 kg that mountain is a killer, and there were a lot of times when I only just made it to the top. Today, the mountain stages are much shorter, so the riders don't arrive so fatigued. The Alpe d'Huez is about more than just survival these days.

In 1989 I was riding for PDM. I remember it quite clearly because it was one of those days when the mountains upset the dynamics of the team. There were four of us, including Uwe Ampler, in a group of between fifteen and twenty riders. As you come in towards Bourg-d'Oisans

there's a small climb, a little kick of around 3 km, just past the reservoir before you drop down to the town. After that the run-in starts, and it can be really hectic, fast and frenetic.

I came back to the team car to get some fresh water before the pace went up. Trying to give out bottles in the run wasn't a good idea, but as we reached the summit of the small climb an attack went away off the front. Greg LeMond, Thierry Bourguignon and a couple of others got clear. Erik Breukink was our man contending for the GC [general classification] – he was the one who could make the podium or even win the Tour – so I knew we had to ride him back into the group but I couldn't do it on my own. I needed Ampler to ride too, but he point-blank refused. He was a fourth-year professional and still quite young to cycling, and he simply said he didn't want to ride. 'Get him up here,' I said to the *directeur sportif*, Jan Gisbers, in the car. 'We need to close this gap or keep it to a minimum to get to the Alpe in a good position.' The riders in the breakaway knew that it was a good opportunity to get rid of some of the GC riders, and they were naturally riding flat out.

I was getting towards the end of my racing career at PDM, but Ampler hadn't become a professional until recently. He'd ridden for his country, East Germany, and was used to being the leader, so taking on the role of helper wasn't for him. I rode Breukink right to the bottom of the Alpe. As he went away, I lost contact quickly but I got into my rhythm and caught up with Ampler 1 km from the end …

If you're riding in the front group, you can make a race with the guys you're with and it keeps you going. If you're suffering and you've been blown out at the bottom of a climb, it's a different kind of pain – it can be really morale-breaking, and it's difficult to keep your focus. Some riders can deal

with the psychological blow – they lose contact with the leaders but don't let it affect them. They get into a rhythm and really bring it back. Others can't, however. There were times when I found it really tough, but I've never climbed off my bike. You have to keep focused and be rational.

When the Café du Colombia team arrived on the Tour, it was clear that they were exceptional climbers. They were certainly better than Hinault and the Tour de France contenders. After their arrival the attacks started happening further out. People used to wait until the final climb of the day, but they always went early and the races became more aggressive and faster. They weren't that well rehearsed at descending, though, and there was a good chance that you'd be picking them out of a ravine on the other side.

I believed that I could get on the podium in the Tour de France but I never made it. I think it was because I was over-raced at the beginning of the season. The Tour of Spain was in April then, and in the mid 1980s I rode for KAS, which was a Spanish team, so it was their focus. I raced the Classics, too, so I'd already done a lot of racing before the Tour and it didn't work well for me. LeMond would ride the Giro really out of shape and get stronger towards the Tour. He was like Armstrong and Indurain: their focus was to start well in France, but I often had other priorities.

Despite that, I did wear yellow, in Stage 9 of the 1983 race. I'd just won the bunch sprint in Pau, which gave me a 1-second lead. The following day, however, was a scorcher and very difficult. I was in difficulty straight away. It was brutal. The first climb was the Col d'Aubisque, and I lost contact in the first kilometre. I was over-heating and not feeling good, but to add to my troubles there were photographers on motorbikes wanting to get a picture of me struggling in yellow. The bikes surrounded me, and the fumes from

their engines made it even more difficult to breathe.

There was so much going on in my head. I was thinking, 'Shat, what am I going to do here? How am I going to walk out this one?' When you're feeling like that you have stay away from the red, so you don't explode. When you lose contact you still have to keep your focus. I had the team trying to talk me through it, saying that it would get better, but by the time it gets better you've lost a lot of time. I could hear a radio from the motorbikes, and it was saying, 'Maillot jaune lâché' ('yellow jersey dropped'), 'perdre contact' ('lose contact'). You get paranoid and think everyone can hear it.

I have virtually no memory of riding the second climb, the Tourmalet, that day. I was usually pretty good at the descent, but when you're suffering that much you don't even try to descend fast. I finished in Bagnères-de-Luchon 10 minutes down on the winner, Robert Millar, but I consoled myself with the knowledge that at least I'd had the jersey for one day.

At the end of the stage, I folded that race jersey up and left the pins in to remind me of the effort of that day. After the race finished in Paris I went back to the team hotel and packed it in my suitcase, then put the case in the car. My car was parked just metres away from the hotel entrance, so I went back in to say goodbye to some of the guys. When I came down half an hour later the car had been broken into. They'd taken my suitcase containing the yellow jersey and my green sprinter's jersey. I called the police, who found the suitcase and some of my possessions in a nearby street, but not the yellow jersey. The Tour de France did send me a replacement, which is framed at home and sits alongside the jerseys from Milan–San Remo, Paris–Roubaix and the other big Classics I won, but it was devastating to lose the one I'd actually worn.

Col du Soulor: the view from the Col d'Aubisque.

Luz Ardiden, where Lance Armstrong crashed – also taking down Iban Mayo –
after a spectator's musette snagged his brake lever in the 2003 Tour.

Luz Ardiden: the road ends at the ski station.

Pyrenees.
Col du Tourmalet.
2,115 m

Geraint Thomas

The first time I was in the break on the Tour during a mountain stage was on the Tourmalet in 2011. When you're in the front group, the crowd are more excitable and louder than when you're at the back. I remember riding at my own pace, feeling good, feeling strong. All of a sudden I was riding on my own, and then I was leading the race.

With a couple of kilometres to go, I saw Jérémy Roy, a French rider, coming back up to me so I waited. As we reached the top Roy sprinted for the line. I remember thinking, 'Oh, ok, whatever. I don't know why he bothered doing that.' Then, later on, I realized that there was a €5,000 prize for the first guy over the top. It was the highest point on the Tour that year, so it was a bit frustrating.

I've raced over the Tourmalet since, and it's always special. Riding through the crowds on a mountain stage such as this is incredible. I grew up watching the Tour, seeing riders like [Jan] Ullrich riding through that noise. As the crowds get thicker, your senses get over-loaded with sounds and colour. You can't hear, and you can barely see the road in front of your front wheel, but I love it. As you leave the crowd behind and ride over the top your ears are ringing, and then suddenly there's this silence, and all you hear are the sound of your tyres on the road and your breath leaving your body once more.

Bernie Eisel

Cav [Mark Cavendish], [Mark] Renshaw and I went through some shit in the mountains. The biggest climb for us was the Tourmalet, which Cav found really hard. It's just short of 20 km long and is an 'hors catégorie' (meaning 'exceptional' or 'unclassified') climb. Even the best climbers find it tough. My job was to help Cav get through these stages.

Long climbs are difficult for sprinters physically but also mentally. Riders are outside their comfort zone, and mountains have a way of exposing weaknesses. I remember one occasion when Cav was struggling and we'd had a heated discussion about the pace. He thought I was riding too fast, but in fact I was going at the same tempo. Climbing can put you in a difficult space: your emotions can take over, and it becomes a battle with yourself. On that occasion we rode in silence on opposite sides of the road, Cav on the left, me on the right, all the way to the top.

We got through and had a good laugh about it at the end. Those are the days that bring you together – a band of brothers.

Col du Tourmalet: the climb continues past the ski station of La Mongie.

Col du Tourmalet: crowds line the route of the Tour de France.

Col du Tourmalet: a sea of polka-dot t-shirts, given away free by the Tour's publicity caravan.

Just Like Home.
Robert Millar

There's a hint of smoke in the distance, and it's a subtle clue as to what awaits the unwary. Moments later, a few reflected flashes of sunlight confirm that it's definitively today's challenge that's sending out signals, even if they turn out to come from self-contained barbecues.

As we get nearer the climb, I can see people and their belongings silhouetted against the dramatic backdrop, like a scene from a Western. In this particular movie they are the bandits, and we are the travelling convoy about to be attacked. Spaghetti was one of the choices at breakfast this morning, but now I'm glad I declined the pasta. If shots are going to be fired, even metaphorical ones, I'd like to believe I've done all I can to have luck on my side.

Some of the natives who await our passage might even be from Mexico or proper Red Indians, but if so they are lost among the more familiar tribes who have invaded every available roadside nook and cranny. In this Alpine setting 'northern' refers to Europe, not America, though judging by the size of the vehicles parked here the New World's motto of 'bigger is better' is winning out. I suppose it's normal: you couldn't bring the compulsory flags, banners, folding chairs and satellite dishes if you came on horseback. And even if you could, one low-level flight from the television helicopter and your steed would be off into the sunset with pots and pans a-jangling. Best bring a van the size of a house so you can be sure you've got everything.

The Belgians and Dutch, who seem to dominate cycling's motorhome scene, like their home comforts in the same way that they like seeing their heroes pedal uphill.

It's one of the unrecognized peculiarities of the Low Countries that a hill of any sort has at least two roads going up it, though if there's enough land available it's usually more. When the roads are finished they build nice cafés and restaurants along the top, and hold races that pass them by in every possible direction. Eat, drink and be merry, with some peloton action for dessert, all in a climate-controlled environment.

It's a popular pastime up their way. No wonder, then, that during their holidays they travel the length and breadth of Italy, France and Spain seeking out similar entertainment in a similar style. And here we are today. The sun is shining, the beers are suitably chilled, and the flags are waving in the breeze. Motorhome life is good, and the modern-days bandits are happy.

Climbing up through the crowds, among the Flemish twangs I hear Italian, French and English voices too. Thankfully the speed isn't yet that vicious, and there's time to take in the sights and sounds of the gathered masses. Fat, thin, tall, short, young and not so sprightly: the motorized travellers come in every shape and size. Some have red features. No bows and arrows, though – just too much sun and, by the looks of their antics, too much alcohol. They'll be glad of their drop-down beds in a couple of hours' time, that's for sure.

Nearer the top of the mountain there's a change in atmosphere, but it isn't just the altitude. There's more order, the parking is structured, the banners aren't home-made, and there's a certain decorum in the enthusiasm. These are the serious fans, the ones who've been parked for days, maybe a week, to reserve their spot – the same one they had last year, and the year before, and the year before that, too. The final spaces are the preserve of the knowledgeable people. Flags flown by these guys aren't just decorations: they are statements. They don't drop litter, they don't leave a mess behind and, most importantly, they remember the time you came past their favourite café in some local race you've totally forgotten about.

As we approach, I recognize one of the crowd from a couple of days ago: he was at the start and had asked for an autograph. It was on a proper photo, not a scrap of paper, and it showed me wearing so many clothes that I looked like the Michelin Man. 'Liege, in the snow,' he'd said: 'Our motorhome got stuck in the ice and we missed the finish.' 'You're lucky,' I'd replied: 'I almost got frostbite that day.' I don't think his English was good enough to understand, but he'd smiled and wished me luck. Now I can see he's offering up a can of Coke, so just before I grab it I throw out one of my bidons in exchange. Fair swap. Everyone is happy.

A couple of hours later, as we're trying to get to the hotel, I spot him again, in a shiny big camper with Belgian plates. He's stuck in the usual post-race traffic jam but he's not driving, which is wise, since he's got his feet up on the dashboard and a beer in his hand. There's a collection of bidons from various teams in front of him along the base of the windscreen.

He winds down the window and waves the beer. 'Cold!' he shouts. 'Just like home.'

Col du Tourmalet: the most visited climb in the history of the Tour de France.

Lagos de Covadonga: beyond the mountains lies the Bay of Biscay.

Asturias, Spain

Lagos de Covadonga	*1,134 m*
Alto de Gamoniteiro	*1,772 m*
Alto de l'Angliru	*1,573 m*

featuring contributions by
Robert Millar, Andy Hampsten

Lagos de Covadonga: an iconic climb of the Vuelta a España.

Lagos de Covadonga: over the crest lie the glacial lakes of Enol.

Narnia.
Robert Millar

As I approach the climb there's a surprising calm. In my memory of my last visit it wasn't like this. Even though I've been at the foot of this mountain many times, today it feels rather different. The first slopes are gentle enough, and I retain enough mental capacity to search for a suitable word to describe the sensation. Serene? No, there'll be pain ahead. Calm? No, too ordinary. Daunting? Scary? The sun is shining and the warmth is building, but the sweat is on my forehead, not my back, so isn't a worrying prelude to what I'll surely experience later.

Welcome.

That's it: 'Welcome.' To nature's theatre. The valley's sides are like dark-green velvet curtains, shielding images of a show that you are about to enjoy. I knew I recognized the glimpse of light that marks the summit from somewhere: it was that infamous Narnia trip. It was a birthday treat (not mine), for which we'd been taken to see *The Lion, the Witch and the Wardrobe*, but sadly I disgraced myself.

In my defence, I had my reasons. I wasn't an indoor child; I couldn't keep still. I noticed things. Details. If there was a question to be asked on the minutiae of life, I saw no reason why my parents couldn't answer it. Wasn't that one of their tasks, after all: to educate me? That was why I was sitting on fold-down velour seats waiting to be amazed by a version of a book I hadn't read. Otherwise I could have been in the park, chasing swans, risking broken arms if I got in their feathery way.

As we sat down in our places they probably knew I'd spot the chink of light peeking through the top of the badly drawn curtains, hoping I'd be overwhelmed by the surroundings. I wasn't. I'd clocked its triangular shape against the dark instantly. Its brightness was far more intriguing than reading the programme or counting how many children were squabbling already.

The simple question of why they hadn't closed the top of the curtains signalled the start of the agony and forever tainted my theatrical experiences. I noticed that the scenes wobbled, heard the actors shuffling in the wings, saw wires holding lights, and heard the squeak of a pulley that needed oil. Worst of all, I noticed that the Lion wasn't a lion. Narnia, the wonderland, wasn't magical at all. It was lacking maintenance.

Which is something that seems to be affecting my left-hand crank, because as soon as I get out the saddle there's an awful creaking coming from down below. It seems that even thinking of the theatre puts the kibosh on things, so with no mechanical sympathy at all I pour water from my bottle on the general area, knowing that that ought to shut it up. The squeaky protests stop. Maybe that's why there's a drinks interval at the theatre, to oil the passages of those who would rather be elsewhere.

It's just as well the noise has stopped, because with a pesky headwind I'm in and out of the saddle continuously, until the gradient eases ever so slightly with the arrival of the few bends there are on this mountain. Though they're not exactly hairpins, the change of direction eases my suffering enough that I can enjoy the view back down to where I've come from. It's certainly worth the struggle, because the scenery is stunning. I can pick out sheep, old refuges, see where streams are winding through the grass and hear a chainsaw buzzing as it cuts branches.

In the far distance I can make out fellow cyclists like little coloured ants, crawling their way upwards, as I've just done, and off to the right there is a buzzard riding the thermals, rising gracefully and without apparent effort. I could do with some of that. I hadn't noticed half of these things before, so I savour the opportunity to study the variety of sights and sounds in this timeless terrain.

A proper corner signalling the second half of the climb brings me rudely back to the job in hand, necessitating some pretty rapid gear changes and a long period of dancing on the pedals. The fateful creaking has resumed, but I'm loath to douse the crank since I figure I need the liquid more. In any case, with the wind whistling in my ears I can't hear it enough for it to be as annoying as it was before. The buzzard can, but the heavy breathing that now accompanies the squeaks obviously does not come from anything resembling a juicy rabbit, so after a while the bird swoops off to observe someone or something else.

With the switchbacks behind me and the top in view again, I get the chance to settle down in the saddle for the final kilometres and have some relative silence. It's almost a relief to be guided upwards by the valley sides that squeeze the road on this last section. It might not be as welcoming as the beginning, but nevertheless the light that seemed so distant now looms large on a slowly approaching horizon, and a feeling of satisfaction starts to fill me. Then – just after the line marking the summit, just when I'm about to launch into the descent – I see my reward: an ice-cream van on the right of the car park. I wasn't allowed a choc-ice in the other theatre, but I am today.

Lagos de Covadonga: for many months of the year the road is impassable.

Alto de Gamoniteiro: transhumance farming in the Asturias.

Alto de Gamoniteiro: the concrete ramps reach a gradient of 18 per cent in some sections.

Alto de l'Angliru: a controversial climb in the 2002 Vuelta a España.

Alto de l'Angliru: steep and unrelenting, the climb is almost impossible in wet conditions.

The Winch.
Andy Hampsten

North Dakota is absolutely flat – Holland-flat. It's in the Upper Midwest, a state in the Great Plains formed from a glacial lake that created a two-dimensional landscape. There's length and breath and a ton of wind, but no depth, no mountains. I started cycling in North Dakota; by then I'd seen mountains, and knew about mountains and cycling, but I'd never ridden them. They were a mystery to me.

When I started travelling as a junior racer I got to spend time in Colorado, where the American Olympic Committee has a base. Colorado Springs is a town on the edge of the Rocky Mountains, and from here we'd have training camps. Riding with the seniors was hard. We'd do local climbs and they'd test us. I wasn't especially fitter than anyone else but, as soon as the rides got steep and a little bit longer, I found that I could climb really well. Those camps laid the foundation for my career.

The older guys would give us advice, instructions on climbing. Relax, let your body work. It was stuff that would stick with me forever. Coming from the plains, where the wind buffets you and beats you up, I found riding in the mountains a relief, even though the workload was still hard, extreme. Battling against gravity somehow seemed easier. Maybe it was because I was light (it gives you a psychological advantage), but I instantly had an edge on the others, especially the non-climbers who struggled from the start of the climbs. Riders who were ten years older than me and racing at the Tour de l'Avenir – guys who were winning national championships – recognized how good I was at climbing, and so I focused on it.

I asked my coaches for hilly rides, and sought out Bob Cook and other great American climbers to ask what I should do and what I should be thinking. For me, climbing became similar to time-trialling, in which I had been told to think of my legs, pedal the whole 360 degrees and not move my upper body. As a skinny guy I had very little horsepower, so everything else had to count. The more I rode, the more I developed my technique, which was essentially just to sit and spin and stay as relaxed as I could.

It didn't take long before I started getting results in races with mountain-top finishes. I remember seeing a kinesiologist a few times when I had knee problems. He didn't know a lot about cycling, and he said to me, 'I hear you're really good at it. When you're climbing, how do you feel? Are you fighting and pushing against something, or is something pushing against you?' I told him it was like trying to break through the resistance, like trying to counter gravity, but above all it was just such a relief that it wasn't windy and that I didn't have to stay crouched over the bike. He found the idea of climbing really interesting and challenged me to imagine that there was a string connected to my chest winching me up the mountain. Initially, I thought it was a bit odd, but I tried it when training and it really helped. During a time trial in the 1988 Giro I needed to protect my lead, so as I started to roll I closed my eyes and thought, I'm going to feel that cord and let it all happen. When things were going well I'd call on that thought, and it worked.

Like most climbers, I like attacking people when they're hurting and have a few kilometres to go. When you're on the attack, you're always trying to find people's weaknesses, which means that you come across as a bit gruff. When you're trying to keep up with someone it's not about making conversation.

I've raced a lot of climbs that I certainly didn't win. So often there were surges in the pace and I'd get dropped. In this situation it's tempting to panic, but I found myself able to calm down even further and to catch my breath. I'd tell myself that they'd soon slow and start to assess each other. If I kept it steady I'd get back to them. And I did. That happened many times.

Later in my career I'd go round Italy and France to perform some of the climbs I did when I raced. I'd go alone and take time to look around and get a feeling of the place. I remember being in races, seeing these incredible landscapes and thinking, 'I need to come back here', but in a race they're gone in an instant. It's a joy to repeat the climbs I did in those Grand Tours, without the stress of a race weighing on my shoulders.

Alto de l'Angliru: the summit.

Coll de sa Batalla: morning light.

Spanish Islands

Sa Calobra	*782 m*
Puig Major	*854 m*
Mount Teide	***2,300 m***
Masca	*1,043 m*

featuring a contribution by
Shane Sutton

Sa Calobra: riders and vehicles compete for space on the narrow road.

Sa Calobra: the official name of the climb is Coll dels Reis but it is generally known by the name of the port village at its base.

Sa Calobra: a mecca for professional cyclists and those training early in the season.

Puig Major: the highest climb in Majorca, often used in the Trofeo Serra de Tramuntana early season race.

Puig Major forms part of the Serra de Tramuntana range, which extends across the north of Majorca.

Mount Teide.

2,300 m

Shane Sutton

Training on Mount Teide is what made the difference between Brad [Wiggins] winning and losing the 2012 Tour de France. After he broke his collarbone in 2011 I thought he'd missed his chance but, standing at the top of that mountain in the months before the race, I changed my mind. I realized that he was ready.

Teide is barren: it's like the moon. At the top there's nothing except a twisted, volcanic landscape, but towards the bottom it's nicely tree-lined and the views are breathtaking. As mountains go it's almost unique: there are very few places where you can ride from sea level to 2,100 m in one go. It's not an 'in your face' climb, but it lay within Brad's range (he rides well at around 7–10 per cent), and it's a climb that you have to endure to appreciate its value.

We'd ride from El Médano on the south coast through Granadilla to Vilaflor. The top section beyond Vilaflor is really special for me: it's where the suffering went on, where we did the real work. It's what made him a winner. I'd be following Brad on a moped like a pizza delivery boy. He'd be low on the bike, and I could see his body working, sense his lungs expanding, taking in the air and letting it go. I'd pull up alongside him, urging him to keep going, but he'd barely register that I was there.

There's a sharp right-hand bend about half way to the top. By this stage of the climb he'd be riding hard, at threshold power, but from here it's still around 8 km to the summit. From time to time I still had nagging doubts. We'd get to this hairpin and I'd be thinking, 'He's going to stop', but he never did. Most people crack on Teide, they pop, but this is where Brad emptied the tank. He'd ride like it was a time trial.

Teide became our world for weeks at a time. We'd stay at the Parador hotel at the top, which means that you're sleeping at altitude but also pretty much stranded. It's totally isolated, eerily quiet and 24 km to the nearest village. Your whole life becomes about getting to the top as fast as possible. All you can do is ride, recover and sleep. I remember sitting there one day, thinking that we'd found a place where we could go deeper.

Mount Teide: clouds swirl around the crater.

Mount Teide: a popular destination for pre-Tour altitude training.

Mount Teide: the road cuts through old lava flows.

Mount Teide: lights from the coastal town of Puerto de la Cruz glow underneath low cloud cover.

Mount Teide: the Parador hotel sits at the base of the volcanic cone.

Masca: houses perch on the hillside, with its spectacular views over the Mediterranean.

Masca: Tenerife's hidden gem.

Giau Pass: one of the most iconic climbs in the Dolomites.

Dolomites & Italian Alps

Fedaia Pass	*2,057 m*
Colle delle Finestre	*2,176 m*
Giau Pass	**2,236 m**
Valparola Pass	*2,168 m*
Sella Pass	*2,244 m*
Stelvio Pass	**2,757 m**
San Boldo Pass	*706 m*
Pordoi Pass	*2,239 m*
Gardena Pass	*2,133 m*
Tre Cime di Lavaredo	*2,320 m*
Gavia Pass	**2,652 m**

featuring contributions by
Tao Geoghegan Hart, Maurizio Fondriest, Allan Peiper, Ivan Basso, Greg LeMond, Lizzie Armitstead, Andy Hampsten

Fedaia Pass: the Marmolada lies to the south.

Fedaia Pass: the lake.

Colle delle Finestre: the summit marker.

Colle delle Finestre: goats block the road.

Place.
Tao Geoghegan Hart

Place I

I travel between worlds that are sometimes dark and damp; moist, like undisturbed morning dew. Sometimes old and familiar, engraved in my mind like the grooves of my palms. Sometimes they are new: a breath of fresh air in every sense. In either case, they are always brimming with lessons to learn.

I pass through dense shadows and freezing air that falls deep into my lungs. I feel my way, the surface of the road rising up through my hands, shaking my knuckles and tarnishing my skin. Occasionally a glare of light escapes through the canopy, a fleeting opportunity to build a sense of where I am. But for the most part I simply pass through, everything falling beyond my focus.

And then my momentum and the twisting road throw me into a patch of light. It warms my body instantly, but the sensation is, like everything, temporary. Again, I see nothing. But I feel. And the feeling is stronger the further you furrow, the higher you venture. Turn away, let go, and the feeling will last for an eternity. There is only one way out: you cannot escape, only go up.

The road starts to lope upward, passive for now. It ripples a little, and my hands loosen to compensate, guiding me forward against nature's will. It cuts a path between left and right, but it serves no purpose but to reach the top, the end. Likewise, as I slow against the gradient, I serve no purpose but to reach the top, someday.

I feel a need to look down from this mountaintop. What is down below is mighty, self-contained. Here it is cold, different, aloof. But it is peaceful. It is a place of its own. A rarity. The city I grew up in is littered with viewpoints, but they are artificial: constructed, created. It's outside this bubble, here in the high up, that I find a clear and lasting sentiment.

Place II

Five hours I've worked, with not a word spoken, barely a soul seen. Her hand rests defiantly on the counter. I see her eyes deepen at first; grooves flaring in all directions sharpen and tense as I reach out. The door swings slowly and heavily on its hinges, reluctant to give way. I push hesitantly again, looking through my hand, past my own weathered skin, watching her. She watches me.

I sense her disappointment that I'm a stranger almost immediately. It is palpable, even through the glass pane of the door.

I remove my glasses and unclip the strap from my chin, a subconscious courtesy of sorts, perhaps. The clock above the counter catches my eye, the time reminding me of life away from these deserted mountain roads and the villages they serve. The second hand ticks tantalizingly slowly, almost impervious to time itself and in keeping with its humble surroundings. I glance outside and away for a moment, towards that distant life. I see sodden stone walls, dripping wet, doors made long before myself, defiantly closed.

I take a seat and now 'remove my cap', along with my outermost layer and the contents of my pockets. My fingers lack sense, so they simply fish around, pulling out anything they can. A coin bounces onto the floor and into a dark corner, lost.

The anticlimax of an unknown guest is heavy in the air, and I sense that strangers are rare. I try to be warm, both outwardly and within, but neither is welcome. The cold has sunk into my bones during the last hours, and into hers, too – but for the last fifty years or more. Her lip remains stout and strong, and an unfamiliar silence echoes in my ears. I wish another coin would hit the stone slabs and cut the nothing.

We speak a few words, broken on my part, and she turns her back. I hear the handle click into place and a slow whir as the machine comes to life. Moments later she approaches bearing a small cup and saucer in her hand, a biscuit resting precariously on its side.

She places it on the scarred wooden table and stands over me in a maternal fashion, a striking contrast to how she was before. My hand immediately searches out the handle. Her eyes stare intensely as I sip, as if watching me spoon in a miraculous medicine. And then, out of nowhere, comes a broad and overwhelming smile, as wide and encompassing as the very mountains I seek refuge from.

Drinking bad coffee is like a long, tortuous climb in training, when the legs just aren't there. It hurts, it's no fun, but it serves as a means to an end. You know how it should feel, but that sensation never quite arrives. But still you become warm, finding a simple kind of solace. In spite of their sometimes arduous nature, both a climb and a mug of dark liquid always seem to clear the mind, even on the worst of days.

In fact, the coffee is not bad. It's soothing, trickles down deep, much farther than I had expected. She continues to smile as she retreats to her place behind the counter top, back to where she began. Her tone has changed and, as I catch her eye, the tension, the look through the door, the cold disappear.

I realize that I am a stranger not just to her: I am foreign to most people. It is not normal what we do, out in that, up in this. I think of the sweaty, gritty, freckled face she saw through her door; the worn, grubby hand reaching deep into hidden pockets and tugging out a sprawl of coins and folded notes; the foreign, husky voice held back by a fogged brain and riddled airways; the hunger devouring the coffee in an instant.

I leave to return to life and she raises her hand, as rested as I am. A wave and smile into my eyes confirm that I am no longer a stranger, despite the barriers that lie between her world and my own.

I travel between worlds, rising up and coming down. But somewhere, high or low, I find my place.

Colle delle Finestre, famous for its unpaved sections.

Dolomites & Italian Alps.

Giau Pass.

2,236 m

Maurizio Fondriest

It was the 1989 Giro d'Italia, and I was riding with the World Road Race Champion's rainbow jersey on my back. I'm not a climber, but I always had this drive, this burning ambition to finish in the top ten on these mountain stages; joining the *gruppetto* just wasn't an option for me.

The Giau came in the middle of a 131 km stage. I was still young and only in my second year as a professional cyclist, but I was riding through my home region and I was World Champion. I knew the roads and I was determined to do well in front of the Italian crowd. My strategy was to attack on the climb so that I'd get a gap, in the hope that I'd finish with the group.

The Giau has a fierce reputation. The lower slopes are really steep – so much so that you're forced to ride out of the saddle. Standing up on the pedals for long periods is really hard: it drains your energy and makes it a really tough climb.

It was raining as we started the climb, but as we got higher the rain got more intense and quickly turned to sleet, and then snow. The clouds were low, the skies moody, and it was so dark that it looked like we were racing at night. As we topped the climb I was in the lead, exactly where I wanted to be.

There's a photo of me on the climb. I'm focused, concentrating on reaching the top, on being first over the summit. My white jersey is blackened with dirt, and the rainbow stripes on my back are barely visible through the snow. It all felt very epic. In the end I finished fourteenth. I came in with Stephen Roche around 3 minutes down on the winner, Flavio Giupponi, but I'd been first over the top. I'd achieved my goal.

Climbing in bad weather isn't difficult, but descending in rain and snow when you can barely see and you're freezing cold is simply about survival, and in a way it stops being a race. This was one of those days you'll always remember. They're not good days; you remember them because you suffered.

Giau Pass: the route tops out at 2,236 m.

Giau Pass: the penultimate ascent in the Maratona dles Dolomites single-day race.

Giau Pass: the jagged limestone peaks are typical of the Dolomites.

Giau Pass: temperature inversion over the valley to Cortina d'Ampezzo.

Valparola Pass: a stunning view south over the Dolomites.

Valparola Pass: the last pass in the Maratona dles Dolomites single-day race.

Battle.
Allan Peiper

When you're not a climber, the mountains are simply about survival. They push you to the edge of your mortality as a cyclist and as a human. Some of those moments – the times when I was at rock bottom – became defining points of my career.

It was 1992 and my last Giro. I'd got away; I'd got 9 minutes on the group. I'd spent 150 km alone, driving, focused. And then they got me, at the base of Monte Terminillo. It was Banesto, Miguel Indurain's team, who'd started riding tempo. They hunted me down and caught me; sometimes being a bike rider is like being a lion.

As the gradient kicked up, I had a flat. The change was quick but I'd cracked. I watched group after group pass me; it was like that feeling you get as a child when you're forgotten or ignored. I'd slipped and lost my grip on the race, but also on my emotions. Joining the last group was a tipping point, and 3 or 4 km from the top I hit rock bottom.

When you're crying you can't breathe properly, and when you can't breathe the crisis escalates. I remember the sense of panic. I remember feeling like someone was slowly crushing my lungs, squeezing out every last drop of air.

What you never see on television is what happens in 'the bus', and the cameras didn't broadcast what happened next. It was Cipollini, a guy I hated one minute and loved the next, whose hand rested on my back and who started pushing me up that climb. That mental space is somewhere the top riders never enter, but he'd been there. He knew the pain I was in. The physical difficulties you can block out, the emotional ones come and go, but in your mind there is a roadblock – a massive, solid wall in front of you. I was fighting with my mental self.

Many of the guys who rode in the bus during the Grand Tour had come the rough way to cycling. We were the English-speakers – riders like [Paul] Sherwen, [Sean] Yates, [Steve] Bauer and [Phil] Anderson; the 'Foreign Legion'. We arrived in France not knowing the culture and not speaking the language, and to achieve success we'd been made to jump through hoops. We'd worked twice as hard to get a place on a team, and that bonded us. In times of crisis we stuck together.

That climb had crushed my ego, stripped me so that there was nothing left to protect me. There were no pretences to maintain. In the last groups in the mountain stages everyone understands that it's a fight, and so guys band together like brothers.

The emotions that evolve from the physical stress of continuously climbing can come out in strange ways. On one occasion I was riding at the back of the bus with Paul Sherwen up Alpe d'Huez. A Dutch supporter jumped out of the crowd to push a Dutch rider. With the rider gone, the guy stopped running and just stood in the middle of the road. I rode straight into him and fell off.

What happened next was a blur. I dropped my bike, chased after him, pinned him up against a brick wall and saw red. I was bashing him, pummelling the guy, smacking him. I was in a daze when I felt Paul Sherwen grab my arm. 'Leave it. Come on, we've got to go, we've got to ride.' He wasn't worried about the man, he was worrying about the time limit; Sherwen would calculate precisely how fast we needed to ride, and on that day he knew we needed every second. I think we just made it that day, after sprinting the last 200 m of the climb. The effort just to finish the stage was immense. I often wonder what happened to that guy.

The 'bus' was like a family: there were jokes and there was empathy. I remember my first year as a pro on Mont Ventoux during the Paris–Nice race. Gerrie Knetemann came past me on the lower slopes and looked me in the eyes as he passed, saying, 'You'll never, ever be a climber.'

In some ways, that day on Ventoux defined my career. I eventually caught Paul Sherwen and then we caught Knetemann, who was at the end of his career. As we passed Gerrie he turned his head. He was red-faced, with sweat pouring off him. Our eyes met and he muttered, 'I'll never be a climber.' He was at crisis point but he still had the capacity for humour. It was one of those moments of camaraderie that can happen only in war. From that day on and for the rest of our careers Sherwen and I called each other 'The Climber'.

The Sella Pass forms part of the Sella Ronda ski route.

Dolomites & Italian Alps.

Stelvio Pass.

2,757 m

Ivan Basso

One of the earliest memories I have of riding a bike is climbing the Stelvio at the age of 8 with my dad. There's a great picture of me on the climb: it was a bright summer's day, warm enough for a short-sleeved jersey, and I was riding my blue-and-silver Francesco Moser bike. The Stelvio is tough for any cyclist, but for a child it's a pretty special achievement; it felt like I was climbing the highest mountain in the world.

The Stelvio is a symbol of the Italian Alps and has a magical appeal to cyclists. It's a bucket-list climb that has to be done and experienced, but it's brutal. Its altitude, length and gradient make it one of the hardest climbs there is. The road was built by an architect called Carlo Donegani, who people joked was the 'designer of the impossible'; it took 2,500 men five years to build, and there are seventy hairpin bends. Visually it's stunning.

For me, just hearing the name 'Passo dello Stelvio' is enough to induce fear. On a climb as long as this there is only one rule: don't go into the red (in Italian we call it 'fuori giri'), especially in a race. Push too hard, even if you're feeling good, and you'll never make it to the top. In the last 5 km you're riding at over 2,000 m above sea level, and there's so little oxygen that you're gasping for breath.

It's rare to see an attack on the Stelvio, because it's so long. When you hit the last few kilometres the gradient is really harsh, and you're riding slow, as low as 8 kph. At this point you've already ridden 20 km uphill, which takes its toll, so it takes only a slight increase in speed before you see riders exit from the back and get dropped. This is a climb that does the culling itself; there's no need to attack.

For a cyclist, it's on the climbs that you become one with the bicycle. Climbing can be an intense, emotional experience but, for me, when you're pushing hard and at your limit, it's the best sensation that you can have on a bike.

I've climbed the Stelvio in situations where I was in the running for the general classification in the Giro d'Italia, and in others when winning wasn't on the cards, so I could relax. The psychological approach to a climb is very different if you're a race contender from when you're simply getting to the top.

When things aren't going well this mountain can be really cruel. In 2005 I was second in the overall standings in the Giro, and I was aiming for the podium or even a win. I'd had stomach cramps the day before and, as I approached the Stelvio, the pain got worse and worse. Every pedal stroke against that fierce gradient was torture. I lost 42 minutes and my chances of winning the Giro were wiped out. On that day the Stelvio really did seem like the highest mountain in the world.

Stelvio Pass: for much of the year the road is blocked by snow and ice.

Stelvio Pass: ice stalactites hang from the tunnel roof.

Stelvio Pass: a favourite mountain of the Giro d'Italia.

Stelvio Pass: 'In the last few bends, I felt I was going to die,' said Fausto Coppi after reaching the summit in the 1953 Giro d'Italia.

Stelvio Pass: riders tackle the climb from Bormio during the Granfondo Stelvio Santini.

Stelvio Pass: the Cima Coppi prize, for the first rider over the highest pass in the Giro d'Italia, often features the Stelvio.

Stelvio Pass: there are forty-eight hairpin bends between Prato and the mountain's summit.

San Boldo Pass: the pass's five single-lane tunnels are governed by traffic lights at each end.

San Boldo Pass: the 'Road of 100 Days' was built by the Austro-Hungarian army and prisoners of war.

High Life.
Greg LeMond

There are no mountains in Minneapolis. It's odd that I live there, because mountains have always been a big part of my life.

At the age of 8 I moved from Los Angeles to Washoe Valley, near Reno. I remember the car drive there, from Los Angeles into the Sierra Nevada mountains: the landscape was so dramatic compared to the city. I'll never forget that journey. Those early years were all about hiking, fishing and camping in the mountains; the crystal-clear skies, the trees, the rocks – they all held a fascination for me. Then, when I started skiing, it was all about going downhill fast.

One summer I took up cycling as a way of staying fit, and I was soon riding 15 km climbs once or twice a week. At that stage the purpose of cycling was to train for skiing, but the following winter there was one of the worst droughts ever. There was no snow, so I just kept riding. I was enjoying the sensation of riding hard and getting wiped out and then seeing how I recovered. Later in life, when I became a pro, it was my ability to recover that helped me succeed; the last week in a three-week-long Grand Tour is where guys fall apart and where the differences are made.

During training I had time to really enjoy the mountains. I would go to the Alps before the Dauphiné or the Tour de France on a ten-day training camp. Somewhere with a lot of ramps to train on made it a good spot. Chambéry was ideal: I could do a different course and different climbs every day.

The difference between racing and training is suffering. When you train, you never push yourself as far as you do in a race, but that's why I loved racing so much. In a race, when the rabbit is chasing the carrot, you dig deeper. It's almost impossible to duplicate that kind of effort in training, and that's why I rode a hundred races a year. When I did train, I trained hard, at 'critical endurance', which is just below your lactate threshold. I didn't believe in training easy, so I'd go out and do intense, seven-hour rides. In the mountains you really test your body, and it takes concentration and focus, so your training has to replicate that situation.

In a race, when you've suffered to reach the summit with the lead group, there's a huge sense of relief. As I popped over the top, I used to think to myself, 'Here comes the fun.' I was never nervous or scared on a descent, and I never thought about getting hurt because I knew my limit. Going down is what I liked most about the mountains.

A lot of people don't understand how important good bike-handling is to making up time on a descent, but it can make the difference. I won the 1986 Tour on a descent. I was in yellow, and my teammate Bernard Hinault, who was in second, went on the attack. I got stuck with Urs Zimmermann, who was in third place in the GC [general classification]; I expected him to chase, but he just sat there and the gap grew.

There was 20 km of valley between the bottom of the Col du Télégraphe and the Col du Glandon, and I knew that if I didn't bridge the gap pretty quickly it would be difficult to catch up by myself. I had to make it back up to Hinault, but Paul Köchli, the *directeur sportif* of La Vie Claire, drove up in the car and told me that I couldn't ride with Zimmermann: 'You must drop him,' he said. By now, Hinault had a minute and a half on me, but he had five or six riders up there working with him, including Ruiz Cabestany and Steve Bauer, and they were riding flat out.

I could see my chances of winning the Tour slipping away. I had to make it back up to the group. As you come down the Galibier and through Valloire, there's a 1 km ramp that leads to the top of the Télégraphe. A few hundred metres from the summit I sprinted as hard as I could, trying to drop Zimmermann. We started the descent, and as we entered the first hairpin I heard his wheels lock up behind me, so I pushed on really hard and flew down the mountain. Normally it's easier to follow another rider down a descent, but Zimmermann was unsettled and I was feeling confident. I came up on Hinault so fast that I surprised him: I'd made up the 90-second deficit and I'd done it in 10 km. For me, it was far easier to make up that time on the descent than on the flat, where there were six guys working together.

Grand Tours are won and lost in the mountains. One bad day and your GC hopes vanish. Although I wasn't a mountain specialist, I was never afraid of the climbs. My physiology was ideal for the Grand Tours: I had VO_2 max fitness in the 1990s, plus I rode for really strong teams, Renault and La Vie Claire. The only riders I had to worry about were my own teammates; when I was at the top of my game I never really believed anyone could beat me other than Laurent Fignon or Hinault.

But I always had real admiration for climbers such as Luis Herrera. He was one of a group of Colombians including Fabio Parra who came over to Europe lacking history and tactical sense, but it didn't hold them back, and as soon as the races got to the mountains they just attacked. They certainly lacked some bike-handling skills and the ability to rest and recover, but they were impressive on the bike. In many ways the Colombians were like us. We came over to Europe with no preconceptions, and there had been no one before us. We carved our own path and probably changed the sport in many ways. We certainly had our own ideas about racing and training.

That said, there was only one rider who was a pure climber. Watching Federico Bahamontes ride his bike was beautiful; he just floated on the pedals and danced up the climbs. Bahamontes, the 'Eagle of Toledo', made a lasting impression on me. He was truly head and shoulders above everyone there has ever been.

Pordoi Pass, with the Sella massif framed in the distance.

Pordoi Pass: the outcrop of the Sass Pordoi, accessible by cable car.

Pordoi Pass: the descent back to Canazei.

Gardena Pass: the slopes are also used for alpine skiing world cup races in the winter.

Gardena Pass: the Sella Ring links the Gardena, Sella, Pordoi and Campolongo passes.

Out of Office.
Lizzie Armitstead

I'm a stubborn cyclist but I'm not a natural climber. The punchy climbs of the classic races are where I feel at home – perhaps because I grew up in Yorkshire, where the hills are short and sharp. When it comes to peaks like the Koppenberg, I know I can get over them and be in for the win: one day of psyching myself up is enough. Really I'm too fragile for stage races, but still I give the mountains a go.

Climbing is an important part of any cyclist's training, whether they are a climber or not. It's how I build my power and, strangely, I enjoy the suffering; riding hard and digging into the depths of my physical ability makes me feel alive. Some of the joy of suffering comes from being stubborn – and as a cyclist you need to be pretty stubborn. That's what got me into the sport. When British Cycling came to my school looking to recruit people to the Talent Team, my friend bet me that I couldn't beat him. I couldn't let that go, and so I raced him and beat him, though not easily. It was quite a fight, but that day changed my life.

Leaving the track to concentrate on the road was an easy decision to make. It's not that I didn't love the smooth boards, the endurance and the high-intensity riding of the velodrome: just that I loved open roads, the scenery and mountains more. As a track rider I felt like I was going to work: the same environment, the strict discipline. I just wanted to be out of the office.

If it weren't for the weather I'd still live in Yorkshire. As it is, I moved to Monaco in 2009, where I climb at least 1,000 m every day, and the weather is a whole lot more reliable. The hills around the Côte d'Azur are much longer and require sustained efforts. Those hills are what made me the rider I am today; they're where I built my strength, and they've been part of my journey.

The Col de Braus is my favourite, and it's a climb I do regularly to test my form. The Braus is steady, never too steep, and towards the top there are some lovely long switchbacks. Look down on the bends, and you can see the riders you've overtaken far below. Seeing them as little specks spurs you on. At the top of the climb is a monument to René Vietto, a French rider who was unheard of before he entered the 1934 Tour de France. He was so good in the mountains that they said he was the 'purest mountain climber' France had ever known.

In my first season as a professional rider, in 2009, I rode the Giro Rosa (then known as the Giro Donne) and managed to snatch the white jersey of the Young Rider classification. It was Stage 3, which was 106 km long, including the climb up Monte Serra in Tuscany. I was in competition with Elena Berlato, a lightweight Italian climber who was 10 kg lighter than me, and we were both fighting to be in white.

The bottom of the climb wound up through the trees. The first section was a series of ramps and flatter sections. Elena was going well, and every time we hit the steeper sections she would pile on the pressure and try to drop me. I was really suffering, and every time the gradient went up I'd lose contact with her back wheel. As the road levelled out I'd claw my way back until I was starring at the back of her shorts.

It was sheer grit and determination that got me back each time she attacked. She should have dropped me, but I found an inner strength that gave me the ability to bury myself again and again. In the end, it was a battle that came down to mental strength rather than physical prowess; I was just better at digging deep. Around 3 km from the summit we looked across at each other and nodded in a way that signified a truce. The road had levelled a bit, and by then she knew she couldn't get rid of me (I'd come back so many times), so we rode together to the top. After crossing the line we hugged, like only girls do, and have remained good friends ever since.

There's a constant pressure in a stage race, especially when you're defending a position in the general classification or a jersey, and with every day the stress increases. It's cumulative, building up and up. You have it with you when you're racing, and it stays with you even when you finish the stage.

My 2015 Giro Rosa was a very different experience. Early in the race there was one stifling hot day, and I lost a lot of time on general classification (I never race well in the heat). Suddenly there wasn't the same pressure to perform, because I knew that I wasn't in contention. I felt I'd been released to ride as I wanted. There was a sense of freedom that came from knowing I could take risks and push it into the red if I wanted to. This time if I blew up the consequences weren't the same.

In the mountains it's the shorter stages that can be the most dangerous, because riders are willing to have a go and stage an attack. In 2015 Megan Guarnier, my teammate, had the *maglia rosa*. The Queen Stage, Stage 7, went over a couple of big climbs (the Naso di Gatto and Melogona), but it wasn't a long day, so everyone knew that someone might break.

I wasn't a threat to the overall general classification, so my *directeur sportif* told me to go in the early break. The idea was to get a gap and then ride for Megan once the front group finally caught us later in the stage. When they did catch us my aim was to make sure Megan kept her jersey, but she was struggling – attacks were going left, right and centre – and it was tense. Mara Abbott, who'd won the race twice before, was looking to get some time back before the final stage, which ended with a 13 km climb up San Domenico di Varzo.

Abbott was piling on the pressure, and Megan was gradually slipping further and further back. I was burying myself, pacing her back each time, going right into the red, to my limit. Every time I thought it was over, they would attack again and I'd drag her back up. It happened four or five times, and each time I had to try harder to ride her back on. Eventually we made it over the top, and surprisingly she was still in contention. We descended well, and Megan kept the jersey. That was a good day at the office.

Gardena Pass: the road heading towards the Sella.

*Above: Tre Cime di Lavaredo: the border between Italy and Austria
once ran through these peaks but now lies further north.
Right: Tre Cime di Lavaredo: the road stops at the base of the three peaks
and has hosted stage finishes in the Giro d'Italia in 2007 and 2013.*

Gavia Pass.

2,652 m

Allan Peiper

'Put on everything you have. It's raining here, but on the Gavia there will be a snowstorm,' said Urs Freuler. The Swiss sprinter was my roommate, and it was the morning of the stage from Valmalenco to Bormio. Sheets of rain were pouring out of the sky like nothing I'd ever seen before. Our hotel was at 1,500 m, so Urs was trying to warn me about what awaited.

I pulled on full-body thermals, a thermal jacket and thick wool gloves. I had a balaclava hidden at the bottom of my rain bag. It was there 'just in case', for those occasions they said never happened, but I took it and secretly stowed it in my jersey pocket. I was embarrassed and didn't want anyone to see. On reflection, it was one of the best things I did that day.

In the valley, after the start, we were boiling. I was wearing layers and layers of clothes, and the sweat was pouring off me. As we hit the Gavia, however, a wall of water engulfed us. First it was rain, then sleet, and then thick, heavy snow. I was at the back, rider 150 out of 160 on the road that day.

As we started to climb, the freezing cold hit me, whacked me in the face. I changed down into my biggest gear just to get my heart rate up and get warm, but the higher we got the worse it became. The road was covered in slush, and for a large part of the climb we were riding on a dirt track. There were guys walking with their bikes, guys at the side of the road terrified, crying. The motorcyclists were slipping off because they couldn't keep their bikes upright. I remember thinking that if they couldn't ride, how could we? It was abysmal, catastrophic.

When you're climbing your mind wanders. I used to have old songs come into my head, old memories pop into my thoughts, but on a day like that I was digging up parts of my soul.

Some Italians had lit a fire in an oil drum halfway up the climb. We stopped and warmed our hands. I took off my sodden gloves, changed them for a green army-issue pair and set off again. I finished thirty-eighth that day; it was one of my best mountain performances. They called it 'the day strong men cried'.

Gavia Pass, its slopes covered in snow.

Gavia Pass: snow ploughs work hard to keep the road open.

Gavia Pass: the descent to Ponte di Legno.

My Greatest Day.
Andy Hampsten

I was in pretty good shape that year, but I always fell ill in the spring, so I went to the 1988 Giro just 'hunting' – to see if I could win. If I couldn't, I'd go for stages. There were a lot of mountain days, but the Gavia stage was the one that stood out. It was short, but sometimes the shorter stages are the hardest.

I'd won the uphill finish in Stelvio two days before, so I knew I was riding well. I was right up there on the general classification, exactly where I wanted to be. I hadn't ridden the Gavia before, but my team doctor, Massimo Testa, had grown up in the area and described it to me pretty accurately. It's a tough climb, much of it unpaved, with switchbacks spaced evenly, but the finish comes after a chaotic descent.

On the morning of the stage I woke up to see that it was snowing outside. I was disappointed but I'd grown up in an extremely cold climate, in North Dakota. I'd ride my bike to and from school in the snow, and my cut-off point for winter training was 20°F [–6°C], so I didn't let the weather deter me from sticking with my plan. I was going to attack on the climb, ride at around 95 per cent and save a good amount for the 25 km descent into Bormio.

The build-up to the climb was horrific. Sleet came down in sheets, and people were terrified. I was terrified. I remember speaking to Bob Roll on the false flat between the descent of the first climb, the Aprica, and the bottom of the Gavia. I told him, 'This will probably be the hardest day of our lives on the bike.' My teammates were drowning me in hot, sweet tea from our team car and asking me if I needed anything. Our director, Mike Neil, was nervous and wanted to know how I was doing. He asked if I had my 'game face on'.

Around 10 km before the climb, shivering under four layers of soaking-wet clothes, I told myself to shake off the self-pity. I studied my competition, like climbers do: Franco Chioccioli, who had the leader's jersey, Erik Breukink, Urs Zimmermann and Flavio Giupponi. It was like a death march: they looked like ghosts. The snow was getting heavier and people were scared but, nastily enough, it encouraged me to push on. 'I'm a bike racer ...,' I said in my head.

It was at that point that I stripped off my leg-warmers and shoe-covers. This bundle of sodden clothes carried back to the car told my team director, Jim Ochowicz, all that he needed to know. I kept on a red, long-sleeved base layer – one super-thin layer on my arms – the blue woollen combined-points leader's jersey and a pair of neoprene diving gloves, but nothing on my head. I was freezing, but getting rid of the rest was psychological and sent a message to my competitors: I was serious.

The team was clever and had prepared musettes with dry clothing for each member of the team; they'd even been shopping for wool hats and ski gloves earlier in the day. The *soigneurs* had flasks of hot tea, too. Before the start, someone had called the little Rifugio restaurant at the top of the Gavia to check out the weather. 'It's blowing snow,' they said. 'And it will be much worse on the way down.'

I was still basing my ride on the descent, not the climb, so I left on my own gloves, which were thinner: the gains that could be made on the descent would be much greater than the seconds you could claw back on the climb, so I had to be able to use my hands going downhill.

Back then, the road to the summit was essen-tially just a track and, apart from the final few kilometres, it was mostly unpaved, which was a real advantage. We were riding on slush, and the soil underneath actually gave better traction than tarmac. It wasn't dangerous, not for a bike racer.

There was some discussion of forming a union with the other teams, but that never happened. My team, 7-Eleven, was leading, and someone shouted from the main group, 'Hey, Andy, you're not going to attack, are you?' As we hit a corner, the gradient ramped up to 14%, the surface changed to dirt and I went – I rode away on my 39×25 with all my rivals watching me go.

As I started catching people along the climb, I remember feeling excited and thinking that this could be the day that I took over the lead. At around 5 km from the top I got my hat and neck-warmer from the team car. What started as sleet had now turned to thick snow, and my hair was soaking and frozen. I wanted to dry it before I put the neck-warmer on. As I ruffled my hair I knocked a snowball off my head. It rolled down my back and, rather than melting, it remained a tight, compact ball of ice. I was so cold that my body heat couldn't even melt the snow. Luckily, in those days I wore Oakley Pilots that almost covered my face, so there was hardly a piece of visible flesh on my body other than my bare legs.

At that point I started to reassess, and won-dered if attacking early on in the climb was the right thing to do. The motorbike rode past with the chalkboard displaying the time splits; some guys were already 2 or 3 minutes down on the climb, so the attack was working.

Near the top I took a bottle of hot tea from the *soigneur* and a plastic rain jacket from my musette, but instead of stopping to put it on, which is uncool for a bike racer but smarter, I wasted time swerving around on the slushy road. By the time I was sorted I had wasted 43 seconds and Erik Breukink had caught me.

As he started to descend, I decided to follow his line. If he slid off the edge I would just go the other way! However, he took the descent really slowly, so I passed him. It was eerie riding down alone. There was no lead car, no team car and no motorcycles. By now it was a white-out, and the visibility was down to 20 or 30 metres. Suddenly, out of the snowy gloom a mechanic from Carrera appeared carrying spare wheels. I remember he wore these beautiful waterproof trousers and coat from their sponsor, Gore-Tex. But the guy was walking up the middle of the road, cursing; he thought the race had been abandoned and he had been left behind. I had to swerve to avoid crash-ing into him. I could hear his shouting fade as I carried on down the descent.

By now I had only one gear (the rest had frozen), and my shins were covered in a layer of ice, but I was done with moaning, shouting and asking God for help. I just had to make it to the Santa Caterina and then another 13 km to the finish. With 8 km to go, Breukink caught me; he must have been right behind me all the time. I couldn't hold his wheel, and my mind was racing with thoughts: 'Is it warmer to put the brakes on and go down this hill at 15 kph, or is it better to go 60–80 kph on this straight 8% slope and risk hypothermia?'

Breukink won by 7 seconds, but that day was my greatest moment as an athlete. I can't put into words what went through my mind, how hard it was, how I terrified myself, and how I suffered like I'd never suffered before.

Gavia Pass: Andy Hampsten sealed his 1988 Giro d'Italia win on the Gavia in atrocious conditions.

Grimsel Pass: the road snakes upwards from the valley floor.

Swiss & Austrian Alps

Furka Pass	*2,436 m*
Grossglockner	*3,798 m*
Nufenen Pass	*2,478 m*
Gotthard Pass	***2,106 m***
Grimsel Pass	*2,165 m*

featuring contributions by
Tao Geoghegan Hart, Bernie Eisel

Furka Pass: once a luxury hotel, this establishment has seen better days.

Furka Pass: the Rhône glacier neighbours the Furka to the left.

Furka Pass: location of a famous James Bond car chase in Goldfinger *(1964).*

The Watch.
Tao Geoghegan Hart

I once knew of a rider who swore he got a job solely because he never raced with sunglasses. His new boss, he speculated, recognized his face among the many. That was enough.

For the tenth time in as many minutes, I check the time. The round face of the watch stares back, dwarfing my skinny wrists, its hands slowing to a crawl. Looking past the seconds ticking away, I feel proud of those wrists, skinny and brown. Lucky, really: I spend an awful lot of time looking down at them, white-knuckled and gripping the bars below.

The mechanic fettling outside seems to drop his spanner every time my eyes close and erupts with yet another chorus of foreign expletives. I try to sleep all the same, sprawled across the back seat of our team van. But as the sun rises into my eyes, the noises outside amplifying in my head, I soon lose hope. Instead, as on most mornings, I slouch off in search of caffeine.

Across a gap between two abandoned buildings vines lope from one wall to the other, hanging lazily in the Sunday morning sunshine. Weeds shoot strong and tall from the ground, sprouting up between the mossy paving stones, each fighting for their own glimpse of sunlight among the busy foliage. It looks like a good life: each plant respecting the other's need for light. A still, tranquil chaos. Something I know little of.

And then they catch my eye through the leaves, a wall of darkness branching across the sky. The mountains: the amphitheatres of my dreams. I focus on their grandeur for a second, my mind wandering up to twisting tarmac and thin air. There are the roads I have been thinking of for months: they have dragged me out of bed as rain hammered on the window, they have driven me out into the cold from the safe haven of my warm apartment. And then my eyes drop to the pavement, feet briskly walking away. I daren't dwell any more on what's to come. I have been dreaming for months, and now they are right here, staring me in the face.

Eventually I find what I set out for, in a small village hall. The coffee is burnt and served in a white plastic cup by an old woman with kind eyes. Perhaps she is already taking pity, aware of the pain the afternoon will herald? I take the cup and a small piece of brioche, and head back towards the team. As I wander, I dip the pastry deep into the cup, searching for solace and homely warmth in the black liquid. For a moment I forget the reality of the day ahead, forget the weight of my dreams and the intensity of those mountains.

A couple more turns of the watch hands and all of a sudden I am lined up at the start – one of a few hundred nervous faces, some staring blankly forward, some laughing nervously and attempting to make smalltalk. The drone of the announcer swirls around the quaint cobbled square. Elbows clash, shoulders bump, the announcer ramps up the volume and intensity, and the day begins.

The race is a blur. My concentration never wavers from what lies ahead, but my eyes are firmly focused on the present, on the wheel in front. Every movement, every breath, is measured, considered. The finale looms large in my mind, as it did in my eyes hours earlier. And it consumes me. I feel it, in my pulse, in my legs. It's like the feeling moments before a first date, over and over, for hours on end.

And then is it right there. Ten kilometres to go. I look up at the road, twisting far up into the clouds, and my stomach finds the next gear in that familiar lurch. I am meant to be a professional; people have turned out to watch us scale this climb, for entertainment – and here I am questioning if I will even make the top.

The gradient bites almost immediately. The pain of the next hour settles into my legs and grabs hold of my lungs, squeezing out the air and the hope from within. The noise of the crowd floats through my head; my eyes, stinging with salt, remain focused on the wheel in front, fixed on the present.

I start to think of my journey here, to this country, this bizarre career: the taxi driver who somehow found the address I had scrawled on the back of one of my mother's brown envelopes; dragging my bags up four flights of stairs; the nightmare landlady; eventually collapsing on the bed, exhausted. It was late and I had been travelling all day, but as I lay there, taking the ordeal in, the bookshelf opposite had caught my eye. It was empty. Home felt ever so distant at that moment.

And as I climb, it feels even further removed. I think of the flat, quiet lanes I grew up in, a million miles from this crazed mountain. Packed close to so many, yet so alone, I am aware that I'm just another face in a crowd. I know how my day will be judged on this tarmac, how my character, my future will be decided according to how quickly I rise through these masses. But what drives me towards the summit are those very feelings from that bedroom, that first night. The bookshelf staring back at me. And so I push long past the point where I should give in, stop pedalling and simply walk away.

The gradient kicks up, levels off, corners and flies up again. A mountain is as much a mental assault as a physical one. I know where the top is: at 212.3 km; the number is ingrained in my each and every thought. But still, at every corner, every false summit, I beg for the finish to appear. I know it won't, but I cling to the hope it might. It's a relentless hour, and I am sure that if I could see the watch its hands would have stopped.

Summoned from the furthest reaches of my psyche over and over during those 60 enduring minutes is a feeling of loneliness, of having to prove myself to everyone and everything, of defiance. And it is this that pulls me, one gasping breath at a time, closer to the top, closer to my dreams, closer to where I think I belong.

Furka Pass: the first dusting of snow on the higher ground signals the start of winter.

Grossglockner: hairpins are numbered from the top down, and this is Kehre *no. 3.*

Grossglockner: the Pasterze Glacier and visitor centre.

Grossglockner: the rugged beauty of the Hohe Tauern range.

Grossglockner: Austria's highest mountain at 3,798 m.

Grossglockner: the cobbled road leading to the hostel.

Grossglockner: owing to its geographical location, the mountain rarely appears in races other than the Tour of Austria.

Nufenen Pass: known to Italians as the Passo della Novena.

Nufenen Pass: the first snow of winter starts to fall.

Nufenen Pass: power lines take hydroelectricity away from the dam at the summit.

Nufenen Pass: the road is relatively new, opened in 1969.

Gotthard Pass.

2,106 m

Bernie Eisel

The Gotthard is one of the nicest climbs in Europe. It's special because they've retained the original cobblestoned surface in the hairpin bends. It's incredible to think of the effort it took to construct: they used dynamite and dug the soil with their hands. I often wonder why they decided to build a road up there.

I've done it so many times – in the rain, in the snow, in the fog – but I'm not a climber, so I'm always nervous about having such a big, hard climb at the beginning of a stage, like we do in the Tour de Suisse. It's tough because the stage usually starts at the bottom in Bellinzona and there's little chance to warm up before you hit the climb at full gas. It's 45–50 kph, then bang, the cobbles, which is a massive shock. We sprinters have a secret weapon, though: we try to block the road so the climbers can't attack at the bottom. It's about limiting our losses but it rarely succeeds.

The Gotthard peaks at 2,106 m, so as you climb you have the altitude to contend with too. As a sprinter you might start at the front but you gradually drift further and further back. The aim is to stay in touch with the group,

or at least the cars. If you lose the cars you're in trouble, big time.

Once you get to the switchbacks at the top it's likely that you'll see bad weather coming in. There's no time to enjoy the view, but there's a minute or so to put on a rain jacket before you start the descent.

The first few corners of the downhill section you invariably do blind. It gets so foggy up there that it can be pretty much dark, even in daytime. Your glasses are usually fogged up too. The descent is about riding fast to make up some time, and that's when the adrenalin kicks in. Occasionally you'll see riders who've reached their limit disappearing into the walls of snow at the side of the road. It's a pretty solid landing but kinda funny!

Geraint Thomas

It was Stage 3 of the 2015 Tour de Suisse, the big mountain stage, and the Gotthard was the first climb. A big chunk of a stage race can depend on the days in the mountains: it's where you make up or lose time, so I was nervous. When

I first turned pro I was still riding the track. I was heavier and I used to dread the mountains; even a 3 km drag was hell. Now that I'm lighter I relish the climbs.

The Gotthard came 10 km into the stage, straight after the neutralized zone. As we followed a long, straight road I was riding right on the bumper of the commissaire's car, which in hindsight wasn't a great move. It turned out that he hadn't driven an automatic car before and slammed on the brakes, thinking he was dipping the clutch. Four or five of us went straight into the back of him and came off.

That wasn't a great way to start a mountains stage. It didn't take long to catch the group again, but when we hit the Gotthard I had no idea it was cobbled; nobody had mentioned it, not even in the race meeting that morning. The surface was not as harsh as the Belgian *pavé*, but it was surreal being on a narrow, twisting climb with hairpin after hairpin covered in cobblestones, the bike shaking all over the place. Once we got 19 km into the race, the climb was done.

I know now that this is what the Gotthard is famous for.

Gotthard Pass: the new road and tunnel.

Gotthard Pass: the view down the valley towards Hospental.

Gotthard Pass: a regular feature of the Tour de Suisse.

Gotthard Pass: the old and the new roads are both clearly visible.

Gotthard Pass: the view at the top towards the dam.

Gotthard Pass: the Devil's Bridge.

The Art of Mountains.
Bernie Eisel

Mother Nature can hit you with shocking force at the top of a 2,000 m mountain.

It's really hard to ride a bike up there at race speed at altitude. We are just a bunch of cyclists heading up there to the top: it's the mountains that hold the real power. I find the environment really humbling.

On the mountain stages I try to keep the *autobus* together, but so much of it is in the mind. Riders in the *gruppetto* can have a really hard time: they're depleted and suffering, and it messes with their heads. Everything is too fast, and they get obsessed by the group's speed. Even the nicest guys get a bit miserable.

It's funny, though: when you get to the top or the end of the stage and you're thinking, 'Thank God that's over,' they come over to thank you for keeping it together. It's become my unofficial role over the years so people rely on me, and it's not very often that we've come in outside the time limit.

These days even the *directeurs sportifs* tell the young riders, 'Stick with him and you'll make the time'; when you hit the big mountain stages in your first Grand Tours you have no idea how to make it to the finish. But it's not rocket science; ultimately it's just pedalling.

There are other factors that can play a role, though – tactics, ways to claw back time – and that's when riding in the mountains is about experience. It might not make sense to an amateur rider, but when it's raining you can make up more time on the downhill than when you're going up.

Some of it you can predict. Looking at the road book before a stage means that you can work out where you're likely to lose or make up the minutes. In my experience you can work out around 80 per cent of what's going to happen, but there's still 20 per cent that's out of your control: crashes, spontaneous tactical decisions within teams, the weather. But, at the end of the day, as long as you keep pedalling you're normally going to make it.

Having said that, there are rules. Everyone has to do his turn when it's flat. If someone misses a turn you know they're having a hard time, but it's not easy for anyone. If a rider is looking for someone to pull them around France, they should go and book a cycle touring holiday.

Descending is one of the best things about being a bike rider. When I was younger we took more risks, but now we make up for it with experience. I reckon I've done the majority of descents in Europe, and I have a vivid picture of most of them in my mind. I know the tricky parts, the sharp corners, where the surprises are, where I need to be a bit quicker on the brakes. Nonetheless, in Italy or Spain you'll often have no idea what's round the next corner.

If you see a bend and there's no guardrail, it's a sign that if you go over it will hurt, but it's not likely to be a cliff or a massive drop. In one Grand Tour I went over the edge and found myself riding along a cow track and then downhill through an Alpine pasture until I hit a massive hole and went over the handlebars. I got up covered in mud and cow shit. I'll always remember that one.

If there is a guardrail and you're going too fast, you have to lay the bike down before you hit the rail. If you hit the rail and go over, you really have no idea what's on the other side; you could go down 60 or 80 metres. It's bad news. That's why you try to crash first. You might break a few bones but you'll survive; you're still alive and not at the bottom of a ravine. It's worth knowing, but it should never get to that point.

Riding in the mountains creates strong, long-lasting friendships; at least, that was the case for Cav [Mark Cavendish] and me. The year I stayed at Team Sky and he went to Quickstep, he said he would never finish a Grand Tour again. I told him that there were enough people in his team who could do what I did, but I think he just felt relaxed with me and didn't have to think. In the mountains Mark knew that he just had to follow my wheel; I would bring him safe and as fresh as possible for the next stage and the sprints. That was our key to success over the years, and it was a type of trust that developed over time. You become very close to your teammates on these stages, and we became best friends. The mountains can make even the most experienced riders vulnerable, but that's what brings you together; you see a piece of someone's soul.

Gotthard Pass: cobbled switchbacks leading down to Airolo.

Grimsel Pass: the Grimsel reservoir.

Grimsel Pass: the rocky outcrop of the Grimsel Hospice.

Grimsel Pass: an aerial view over the two reservoirs.

Grimsel Pass: switchbacks wind through the granite landscape.

Grimsel Pass: 100 million cubic metres of water are held back behind the concrete dam.

References

Maps

Climb Profiles

Teeth.
Allan Peiper

It's probably the most embarrassing moment of my career. It was during one of those hard mountain stages in the Giro d'Italia when it was freezing cold and snowing really, really hard. The day before we'd been over the Marmolada, and on this stage we went back up the other side.

As we came down the mountain it was so cold. There was a Colombian guy who was absolutely freezing, he had no arm-warmers and no jacket. He was shaking so much that he could hardly hold his handlebars, whereas I had so many clothes on that I looked like the Michelin Man, so I gave him my spare hat.

I got down to the bottom and just managed to get onto the back of the last group when I saw that there were two Panasonic riders up the front. I remember thinking, 'What are those clowns doing up there?' It was only 40 km to the finish so there was no need to ride fast. When I looked again, I saw that they were taking turns on the front, so I figured that there was something going on. Our guy, [Erik] Breukink, hadn't made the front group – he was still wiped out from the day before when he'd bonked and lost the lead to Andy Hampsten – but I knew I had to get him up there. I gave it everything and rode with him on my wheel to bring him back to the bunch.

With Breukink safely installed I went back to the car to get a muesli bar, but then it kicked off at the front and the pace went up again. Because it was so cold, the bar had shrunk and was rock hard; I was gasping for breath in an effort to chew it. I decided to give up on the bar and spat it out, but my front teeth came out too! Losing my teeth had always been one of my life-long fears. When I was 13 years old I was elbowed in the face playing football and lost my three front teeth. I'd had a plate put in my mouth and those teeth meant everything to me. There was no way I wasn't go back to get them.

I slammed on my brakes and did a U-turn. I was riding against the traffic, with two lanes of team cars and police motorbikes coming straight at me. And then I saw them, my teeth, lying in the road. I was hell bent on getting them back, but the second I got there, boom! The Carrera team car ran right over them.

I remember the sense of panic. I needed my teeth…I stopped in the middle of road wondering what to do. A second later my team car rolled up next to me but headed in the opposite direction, towards the finish, like I should have been. Peter Post, the Panasonic *directeur sportif*, shouted from the car, 'What the hell are you doing here?'

'I lost my teeth,' I mumbled. He started shouting, 'Get back in the bunch!' so I turned around and started chasing back on. He seemed really angry, but apparently everyone in the car laughed all the way to the finish. The mechanic was hanging out of the back laughing so hard that he was shaking. I was really embarrassed about what had happened.

The next day we were snowed in, so we ate three meals in the hotel. There were twenty of us together at the table, and they kept giving me bananas and soft things to eat. By then the whole team knew and they all found it really funny. Jean-Paul van Poppel just couldn't stop laughing, but when he laughed I laughed, and everyone could see the gap in my mouth. The waitresses were laughing, and in the end the whole restaurant, all the other teams joined in. Everyone. It's probably one of the things that I'm most famous for.

Rider Biographies

In 2015 **Lizzie Armitstead** won the World Road Race Championships and the British Road Race Championships. Born in Otley, Yorkshire, Armitstead began cycling with the British Cycling Talent Team. Her career started on the track, and in 2009 she won five track World Championship medals. Since 2009 Armitstead has concentrated on the road, and she currently rides for the Dutch-based Boels–Dolmans team. Armitstead is not a pure climber, preferring the short, sharp inclines of the one-day Classics. In 2015 she came second in the Tour of Flanders, and she began the 2016 season with a win at Omloop Het Nieuwsblad.

Romain Bardet quickly rose through the ranks of French junior cycling and turned professional in 2012. Known for his climbing ability, in 2014 he placed sixth in the Tour de France. Four years into his career, he had already won mountain stages in the Tour de France and the Critérium du Dauphiné. His fearless descent of the Col du Glandon in Stage 18 of the 2015 Tour gave a big enough lead to win the stage and, albeit temporarily, the polka-dot jersey.

The Canadian cyclist **Michael Barry** was one of the first super domestiques, whose sole job is to ride and support their team leaders in Grand Tours. During his thirteen-year career, he rode in support of Mark Cavendish and Sir Bradley Wiggins on highly successful professional cycling teams, including T-Mobile, Colombia–HTC and Team Sky. Barry also formed part of Lance Armstrong's US Postal Service team. He completed both the Vuelta a España and the Giro d'Italia five times but rode the Tour de France only once, in 2010, two years before he retired.

Ivan Basso retired in 2015 having been a professional cyclist since 1998. The Italian rider rode for eight professional cycling teams, including Team CSC, Discovery Channel and Tinkoff-Saxo. Basso's reputation was forged in the Giro d'Italia, which he won twice, in 2006 and 2010. As a climber, he excelled in the mountains and won six individual stages of the Giro over the course of his career. Basso also completed the Tour de France seven times, coming second in the general classification in 2005.

Bernie Eisel has been a professional cyclist since 2001. He joined T-Mobile in 2007 as a domestique, with the specific responsibility of looking after Mark Cavendish in the mountain stages of Grand Tours. Eisel followed Cavendish to HTC–High Road and subsequently to Team Sky, where he was a key part of the sprinter's lead-out train. Born in Austria, Eisel is known for driving the autobus on long mountain climbs and is considered a reliable wheel. He prides himself on never having missed the time cut.

Maurizio Fondriest was born in Trento, Italy, and won the World Road Race Championship in 1988 at the age of 23, in what was only his second season as a professional rider. During his eleven-year career he became known as a stylish cyclist who knew when to attack and had the tenacity make a break stick. In the mountains he would ride away from the peloton just so that he could be first over the top. Fondriest also excelled in the Spring Classics and early season races, winning the Milan–San Remo, Flèche Wallonne and Tirreno–Adriatico all in the same year, 1993.

In 1986 the American **Greg LeMond** became the first non-European professional cyclist to win the Tour de France. LeMond was considered an all-rounder but was also recognized as a talented climber; he had grown up on the eastern slopes of the Sierra Nevada mountain range in the western US. In the 1989 Tour de France, LeMond attacked time and time again on the Col d'Izoard to snatch the yellow jersey back from Laurent Fignon. LeMond was the first American to win the elite Road World Championship and the first professional cyclist to sign a million-dollar contract.

Robert Millar was the first English-speaking rider to win the King of the Mountains classification in the Tour de France, in 1984. While still an amateur, Millar won the Scottish Hill Climb Championship in 1977. He turned professional in 1980 and quickly established himself as an exceptional climber. During his Tour de France debut in 1983, Millar took his first stage win on a day when the race crossed the Aubisque, Tourmalet, Aspin and Peyresourde in the Pyrenees. In 1987 he won the polka-dot King of the Mountains jersey in the Giro d'Italia. He rode the Tour de France eleven times in total, completing the race eight times, and is one of only four Britons to have won a Tour de France jersey competition.

Allan Peiper was a Classics specialist who competed in the Tour de France five times. He raced throughout the 1980s and early 1990s alongside Stephen Roche, Sean Yates and Robert Millar. Born in Australia, Peiper moved to France in 1982 to race, and the following year he joined the Peugeot cycling team. Peiper's strength as a rider was in one-day races, and by his own admission he found climbing tough. He regularly rode the mountain stages in the autobus (the last group on the road).

The Irishman **Stephen Roche**, a former professional cyclist, is best known for having won the Triple Crown, coming first in the Giro d'Italia, the Tour de France and the World Road Race Championships during the same year. His 1987 Tour de France win featured an epic battle with the Spanish rider Pedro Delgado. On a mountain stage that ended at La Plagne, Roche chased the Spaniard so hard that he needed oxygen at the finish line, but the performance won him the Tour. After thirteen years in the pro peloton, he retired in 1993, with fifty-eight career wins to his name.

Former British professional cyclist **Paul Sherwen** competed in seven editions of the Tour de France during the late 1970s and 1980s. He completed five Tours and developed a reputation for his precise time-keeping on mountain stages, often finishing just seconds ahead of the cut-off time. Sherwen was noted for his tenacity and forbearance in the mountains; after an early crash during Stage 11 of the 1985 Tour, he rode solo for six hours over six mountains. He finished twenty-three minutes outside the cut-off and was technically eliminated from the race, but later reinstated as a result of his courage and stamina.

Australian cyclist **Shane Sutton** moved to Britain in 1984 to race as a professional. He rode the 1987 Tour de France with ANC-Halfords and, after retiring, began work with the British National Governing Body for cycle sport. He is currently Technical Director for British Cycling. Sutton worked closely with Sir Bradley Wiggins throughout his career and particularly in the lead up to the 2012 Tour de France, which Wiggins won. He credits Wiggins's success in part to the time they spent training on Mount Teide, Tenerife.

Geraint Thomas was born in Cardiff. He rides for Team Sky and represented Great Britain on the track in the 2008 Beijing Olympics and the 2012 London Olympics. Thomas turned professional in 2006, and in 2007 he was the youngest rider to compete in the Tour de France. He has had success in the one-day Classics, winning the 2015 E3 Harelbeke and finishing third in Gent–Wevelgem. Thomas worked for his teammate Chris Froome during the 2015 Tour de France, most significantly on Stage 10 in the Pyrenees, when he helped set up Froome's winning attack.

Index

Maps

French Alps

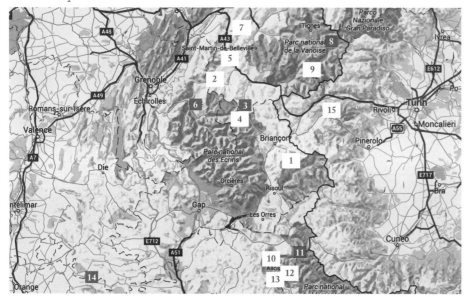

Pyrenees

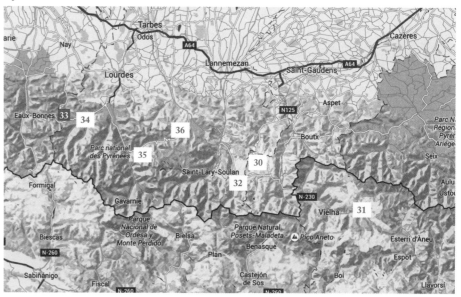

Dolomites and Italian & Swiss Alps

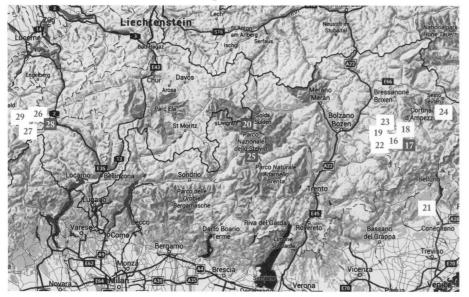

Key

1	Col d'Izoard	19	Sella Pass
2	Col de la Croix de Fer	20	**Stelvio Pass**
3	**Col du Galibier**	21	San Boldo Pass
4	Col du Lautaret	22	Pordoi Pass
5	Lacets de Montvernier	23	Gardena Pass
6	**Alpe d'Huez**	24	Tre Cime di Lavaredo
7	Col de la Madeleine	25	**Gavia Pass**
8	**Col de l'Iseran**	26	Furka Pass
9	Mont Cenis	27	Nufenen Pass
10	Col d'Allos	28	**Gotthard Pass**
11	**Col de la Bonette**	29	Grimsel Pass
12	Col de la Cayolle		
13	Col des Champs	30	Port de Balès
14	**Mont Ventoux**	31	Port de la Bonaigua
15	Colle delle Finestre	32	Col de Peyresourde
		33	**Col d'Aubisque**
16	Fedaia Pass	34	Col du Soulor
17	**Giau Pass**	35	Luz Ardiden
18	Valparola Pass	36	**Col du Tourmalet**

Asturias

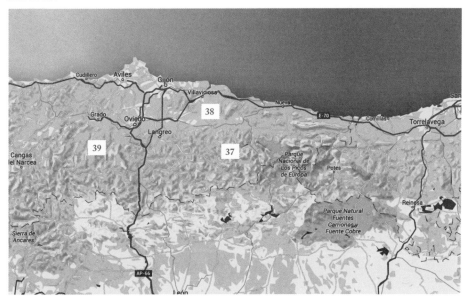

Tenerife

Majorca

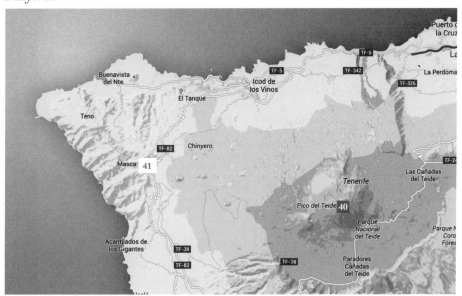

Key

37 Lagos de Covadonga
38 Alto de Gamoniteiro
39 Alto de l'Angliru

40 **Mount Teide**
41 Masca

42 Sa Calobra
43 Puig Major

French Alps

Col du Galibier
(from Col du Lautaret)

The Col du Galibier is one of the most renowned and historic climbs in cycling. Named after Le Grand Galibier, the mountain peak that sits atop the Col at 3,228 m, it is one of the highest and most challenging roads ridden by cyclists in Europe. The high altitude means that snow clings to the northern slopes throughout the summer.

HEIGHT: .... 2,646 m

LENGTH: .... 8.52 km

ALTITUDE GAIN: .... 585 m

AVERAGE GRADIENT: 6.9%

MAXIMUM GRADIENT: 12.1%

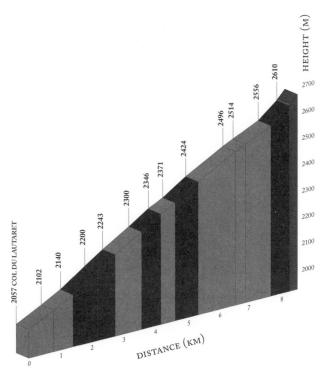

Col du Galibier
(from Châtelard)

• On the first occasion that the Tour de France climbed the mountain, in 1911, only three riders reached the peak without walking.

• All three routes up the Col du Galibier feature another climb on the way up.

HEIGHT: .... 2,646 m

LENGTH: .... 34.9 km

ALTITUDE GAIN: .... 1,928 m

AVERAGE GRADIENT: 5.52%

MAXIMUM GRADIENT: 8.5%

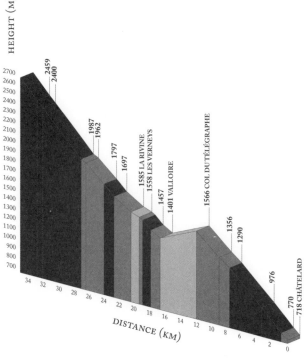

Mont Ventoux
(from Malaucène)

Mont Ventoux – also known as the 'Giant of Provence' – is battered by strong winds from the north, which regularly reach over 90 kph and make the tough ascent even more challenging. In fact, it is one of the windiest places on earth. The bare summit of this limestone monolith dominates the landscape and is visible from as far as 50 km away.

HEIGHT: .... 1,912 m

LENGTH: .... 21.2 km

ALTITUDE GAIN: .... 1,515 m

AVERAGE GRADIENT: 7.15%

MAXIMUM GRADIENT: 10.9%

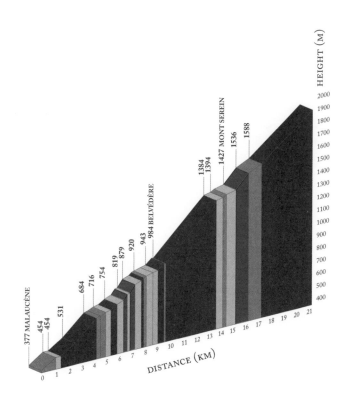

Mont Ventoux
(from Bédoin)

• Ventoux was once covered in thick forest, but demand from the ship-building industry in Toulon led to logging in the 12th century. Ventoux was subsequently nicknamed the 'Bald Mountain'.

• On the summit is a meteorological observatory built in 1882. It fell into disrepair following World War I, before a new edifice was constructed in 1968.

HEIGHT:	1,912 m
LENGTH:	21.5 km
ALTITUDE GAIN:	1,552 m
AVERAGE GRADIENT:	7.22%
MAXIMUM GRADIENT:	12%

Col de l'Iseran
(from Bonneval-sur-Arc)

Although first used in the Tour de France in 1938, the Iseran has featured only six times, most recently in 2007, when the Ukrainian cyclist Yaroslav Popovych led the race over the crest.

HEIGHT:	2,770 m
LENGTH:	13.4 km
ALTITUDE GAIN:	977 m
AVERAGE GRADIENT:	7.3%
MAXIMUM GRADIENT:	10.5%

Col de l'Iseran
(from Bourg-Saint-Maurice)

• It is a 48 km journey from Bourg-Saint-Maurice to the summit of the Col de l'Iseran. At 2,770 m, the Iseran is the highest paved mountain pass in the Alps and is open only in the summer months. Its summit lies 10 km to the east of the Italian border.

• Originally a mule pass, the road was officially opened in 1937, having taken thirty-four years to complete.

HEIGHT:	2,770 m
LENGTH:	48 km
ALTITUDE GAIN:	1,955 m
AVERAGE GRADIENT:	4.1%
MAXIMUM GRADIENT:	6.9%

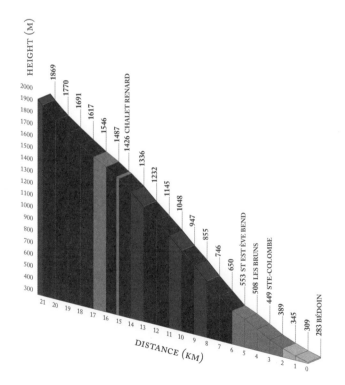

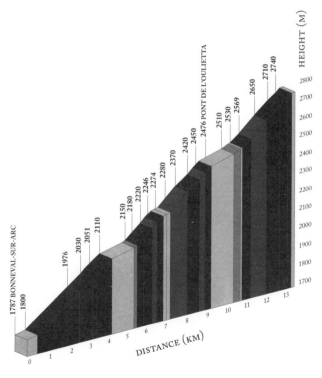

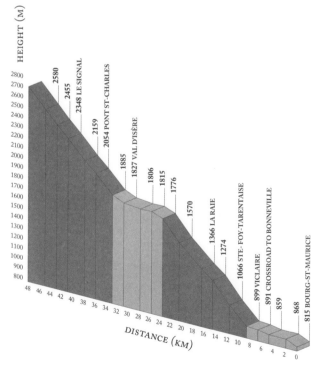

French Alps

Col de la Bonette
(from Jausiers)

The Col de la Bonette in the Mercantour National Park climbs as high as 2,715 m. However, a loop at the top, the Cime de la Bonette, rises up to 2,860 m, making it the highest road (not pass) in Europe.

HEIGHT:	2,715 m
LENGTH:	23.4 km
ALTITUDE GAIN:	1,589 m
AVERAGE GRADIENT:	6.76%
MAXIMUM GRADIENT:	15%

Col de la Bonette
(from Saint-Étienne-de-Tinée)

• The Col de la Bonette is the last great climb of the Southern Alps and marks the route to the Côte d'Azur.

• On the 2008 Tour, the South African John-Lee Augustyn crashed over the edge shortly after starting the descent. He had been leading but spent minutes clambering back up the screed slopes to where his bike lay.

HEIGHT:	2,715 m
LENGTH:	25.8 km
ALTITUDE GAIN:	1,658 m
AVERAGE GRADIENT:	6.4%
MAXIMUM GRADIENT:	15%

Alpe d'Huez
(from Bourg-d'Oisans)

A relative newcomer to the Tour, the Alpe, with its twenty-one hairpins, has become an icon. Its inauguration in 1952 coincided with the first appearance of television crews on motorbikes, which helped bring the drama of the Grand Boucle to a wider audience. Each hairpin is named after a winner of a Tour de France stage. The most popular is the seventh, or 'Dutch Corner', which during the Tour is besieged by fans.

HEIGHT:	1,860 m
LENGTH:	13.1 km
ALTITUDE GAIN:	1,073 m
AVERAGE GRADIENT:	8.19%
MAXIMUM GRADIENT:	12%

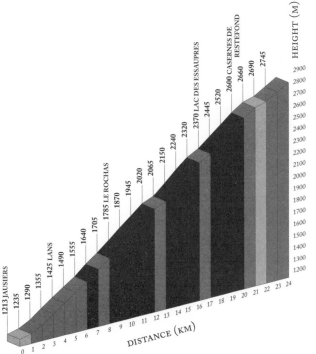

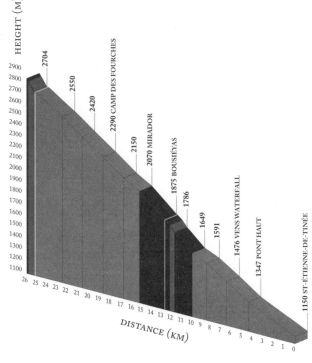

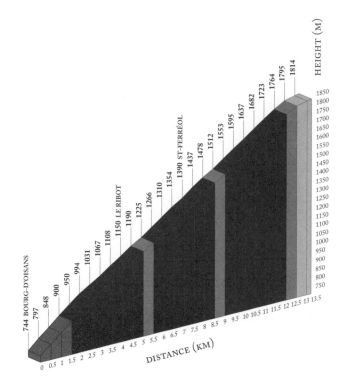

Spanish Islands

GRADIENTS

░ 0–5%	▓ 8–10%
▢ 5–8%	■ 10% +

Mount Teide
(from El Médano)

This dormant volcano on Tenerife peaks at over 3,600 m, making it the highest point in Spain. It last erupted in 1909 and is widely considered as structurally unstable. Its popularity as a winter training ground for Pro Tour teams means that there is fierce competition for rooms at the Parador, the only hotel in the Teide National Park.

HEIGHT: 2,325m

LENGTH: 51km

ALTITUDE GAIN: 2,325m

AVERAGE GRADIENT: 4.6%

MAXIMUM GRADIENT: 8.1%

Mount Teide
(from Puerto de la Cruz)

• To the original Berber inhabitants of the Canary Islands, Teide was sacred. Legend has it that the devil kidnapped Magec, the god of light, and held him prisoner inside the volcano, plunging the world into darkness.

• Measured from its base on the ocean floor, Teide is the third-highest island volcano in the world. Seismic activity has increased significantly since 2003.

HEIGHT: 2,325m

LENGTH: 46.7km

ALTITUDE GAIN: 2,315m

AVERAGE GRADIENT: 5%

MAXIMUM GRADIENT: 7.5%

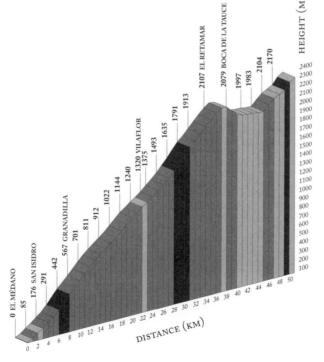

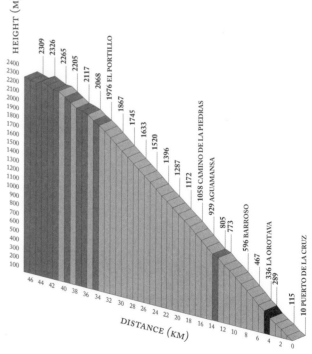

Pyrenees

GRADIENTS
0–5%
5–8%
8–10%
10% +

Col d'Aubisque
(from Laruns)

One of cycling's go-to climbs, the Col d'Aubisque is second only to the Col du Tourmalet as the most visited climb in the history of the Tour de France. The mountain can be ascended from either Argelès-Gazost in the west or Laruns in the east, and peaks at 1,709 m.

HEIGHT:	1,709 m
LENGTH:	16.6 km
ALTITUDE GAIN:	1,190 m
AVERAGE GRADIENT:	7.2%
MAXIMUM GRADIENT:	13%

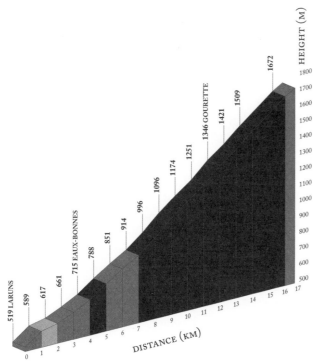

Col d'Aubisque
(from Argelès-Gazost)

• The summit of the Col is marked by a monument to André Bach, president of the Béarn Cyclo Club and a recipient of the Legion of Honour. He died in 1945 while returning from Buchenwald concentration camp.

• In the 1951 Tour, the Dutchman Wim van Est fell 70 m into a ravine while descending the mountain. He was winched to safety by forty bicycle tyres strung together.

HEIGHT:	1,709 m
LENGTH:	30.1 km
ALTITUDE GAIN:	1,247 m
AVERAGE GRADIENT:	4.1%
MAXIMUM GRADIENT:	12%

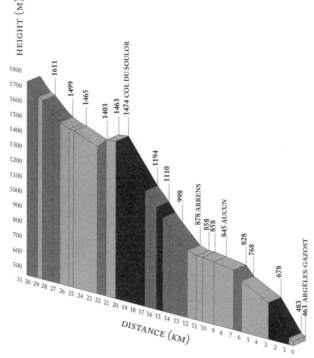

Col du Tourmalet
(from Luz-Saint-Sauveur)

The Col du Tourmalet peaks at 2,115 m, making it the highest paved mountain pass in the Pyrenees. It is the most visited climb in the history of the Tour de France. From the top of the Tourmalet – a Gascon name that translates as 'the distant mountain' – a dirt track continues to climb up towards the Col de Laquets, which sits at 2,637 m altitude.

HEIGHT:	2,115 m
LENGTH:	18.8 km
ALTITUDE GAIN:	1,405 m
AVERAGE GRADIENT:	7.4%
MAXIMUM GRADIENT:	13%

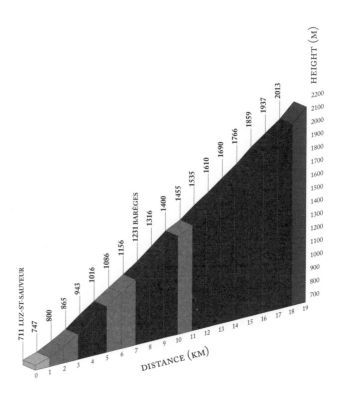

0–5% 8–10%
5–8% 10% +

Swiss Alps

Col du Tourmalet
(from Sainte-Marie-de-Campan)

• The first time riders in the Tour de France crossed the Tourmalet was back in 1910, when the climb formed part of a mammoth 326 km stage.

• The great Spanish climber Federico Bahamontes, known as the 'Eagle of Toledo', led the Tour de France over the summit on four occasions. In 1954 he even stopped for an ice cream to let the others catch up.

HEIGHT:	2,115 m
LENGTH:	17.2 km
ALTITUDE GAIN:	1,268 m
AVERAGE GRADIENT:	7.4%
MAXIMUM GRADIENT:	13%

Gotthard Pass
(from Airolo)

Providing a vital connection between Northern and Southern Europe, a pass through the central Alps has existed here since early medieval times. The road, named after a local 12th-century hospice, was widened and improved in 1830. It now connects Airolo in the Italian-speaking canton of Ticino with the German-speaking canton of Uri.

HEIGHT:	2,106 m
LENGTH:	12.7 km
ALTITUDE GAIN:	932 m
AVERAGE GRADIENT:	7.3%
MAXIMUM GRADIENT:	11.4%

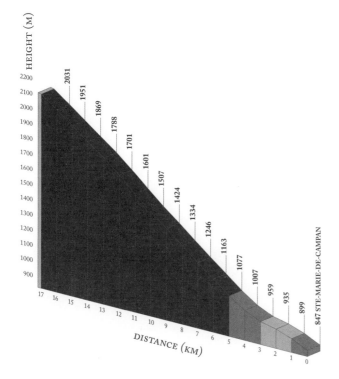

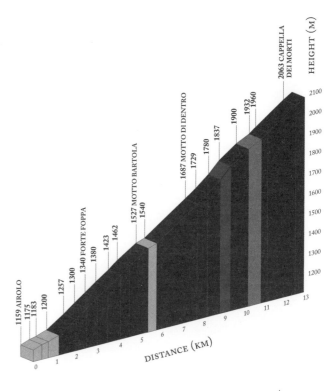

Dolomites & Italian Alps

Giau Pass
(from Selva di Cadore)

A pass rising to 2,236 m, the Giau connects Cortina d'Ampezzo with Colle Santa Lucia in the Dolomites. With an average gradient of over 9% and twenty-nine hairpins, the climb from Selva di Cadore is a favourite of the Giro d'Italia. It was first tackled by the Giro in 1973, when it was still unpaved. The occasion was marked by a fearsome battle between José Fuente and Franco Bitossi.

HEIGHT:	2,236 m
LENGTH:	10.12 km
ALTITUDE GAIN:	922 m
AVERAGE GRADIENT:	9.1%
MAXIMUM GRADIENT:	10.4%

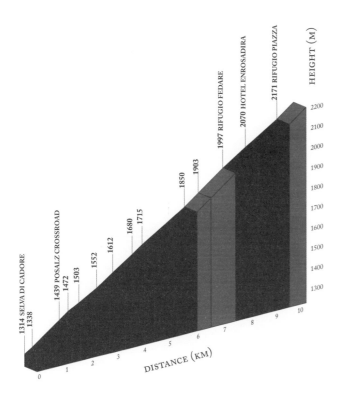

Gavia Pass
(from Bormio)

The Gavia is one of the highest and toughest climbs of the Italian Alps. The drop from the side of the narrow, twisting road – open only in high summer – can be incredibly steep, making the descent treacherous at times. On the south side there is a renowned tunnel that plunges riders into disorientating darkness 3 km from the top.

HEIGHT:	2,652 m
LENGTH:	25.6 km
ALTITUDE GAIN:	1,404 m
AVERAGE GRADIENT:	5.5%
MAXIMUM GRADIENT:	11%

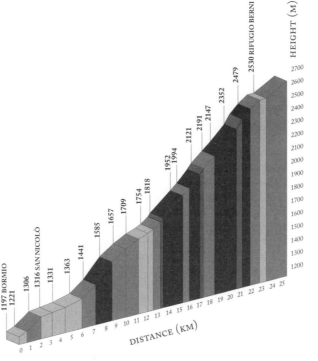

Gavia Pass
(from Ponte di Legno)

- Rising above the pass is the Corno dei Tre Signori, a 3,360 m peak that casts a shadow over two glacial lakes: Lago Nero and Lago Bianco. According to local legend, they represent young lovers forced to separate.

- The Gavia Pass had its most famous day in the 1988 Giro d'Italia, which saw Andy Hampsten's epic fight to take the pink jersey in freezing conditions.

HEIGHT:	2,652 m
LENGTH:	17.3 km
ALTITUDE GAIN:	1,363 m
AVERAGE GRADIENT:	7.9%
MAXIMUM GRADIENT:	16%

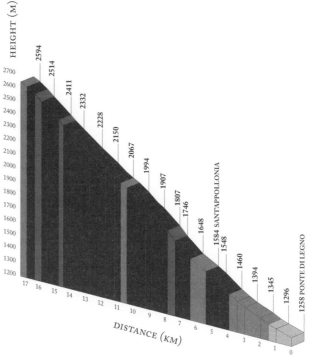

0–5% 8–10%
5–8% 10% +

Stelvio Pass
(from Bormio)

The Stelvio boasts forty-eight hairpins between Prato and the summit. The second-highest paved pass in the Italian Alps, the road is impassable for much of the year. Even in May, during the Giro d'Italia, riders can face tough winter conditions, and the pass is often flanked by high walls of snow. A route over the Stelvio has existed since the Middle Ages, but the road was built between 1820 and 1825.

HEIGHT: .... 2,757 m

LENGTH: .... 21.9 km

ALTITUDE GAIN: .... 1,560 m

AVERAGE GRADIENT: 7.12%

MAXIMUM GRADIENT: 14%

Stelvio Pass
(from Ponte di Stelvio)

• During World War I, the slopes of the Stelvio were the scene of battles between the Italians and the Austrians. After the armistice, both sides of the mountain became Italian. A monument to the fallen stands near the summit.

• Fausto Coppi's ascent of the Stelvio on its inaugural inclusion in the 1953 Giro d'Italia saw him steal the lead from the favourite, the Swiss Hugo Koblet.

HEIGHT: .... 2,757 m

LENGTH: .... 24.3 km

ALTITUDE GAIN: .... 1,808 m

AVERAGE GRADIENT: 7.4%

MAXIMUM GRADIENT: 9.2%

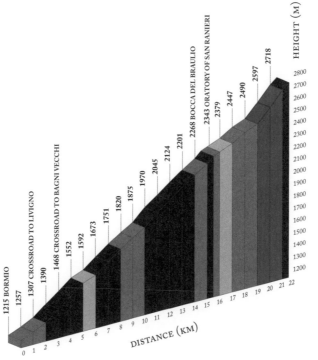

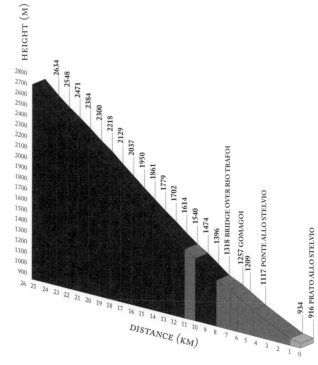

p1: Storm in the Dolomites
p2: Hairpin bend on the Stelvio Pass
p4: The view from Mont Ventoux over Provence

First published in the United Kingdom in 2016 by Thames & Hudson Ltd,
181A High Holborn, London WC1V 7QX

Mountains: Epic Cycling Climbs © 2016 Michael Blann

Photographs © 2016 Michael Blann

Edited by Susannah Osborne
Designed by Andrew Diprose

British Library Cataloguing-in-Publication Data
A catalogue record for this book is available from the British Library

ISBN 978-0-500-51891-5

Printed and bound in China by Everbest Printing

To find out about all our publications, please visit **www.thamesandhudson.com**.
There you can subscribe to our e-newsletter, browse or download our current
catalogue, and buy any titles that are in print.